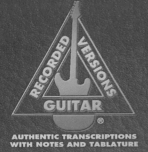

FOLK-ROCK GUITAR BIBLE

AUTHENTIC TRANSCRIPTIONS
WITH NOTES AND TABLATURE

2   AT SEVENTEEN—Janis Ian

14   BEST OF MY LOVE—The Eagles

22   BLACKBIRD—The Beatles

26   CHICAGO—Graham Nash

31   CRYING—Don McLean

36   DARK HOLLOW—Grateful Dead

43   DO YOU BELIEVE IN MAGIC—

49   DOCTOR, MY EYES—Jackson Browne

57   EIGHT MILES HIGH—The Byrds

65   FIRE AND RAIN—James Taylor

70   HAPPY TOGETHER—The Turtles

75   HELP ME MAKE IT THROUGH THE NIGHT—Kris Kristofferson

81   HERE COMES THE SUN—The Beatles

86   IF I HAD A HAMMER (THE HAMMER SONG)—Peter, Paul & Mary

89   JUST A SONG BEFORE I GO—Crosby, Stills & Nash

93   LAST NIGHT I HAD THE STRANGEST DREAM—Simon & Garfunkel

98   LEADER OF THE BAND—Dan Fogelberg

104 LEAVING ON A JET PLANE—Peter, Paul & Mary

108 ME AND BOBBY MCGEE—Kris Kristofferson

117 NORWEGIAN WOOD (This Bird Has Flown)—The Beatles

124 OH, LONESOME ME—Neil Young

131 OUR HOUSE—Crosby, Stills, Nash & Young

134 REASON TO BELIEVE—Tim Hardin

137 SHE'D RATHER BE WITH ME—The Turtles

141 SWEET BABY JAMES—James Taylor

147 TAKE ME HOME, COUNTRY ROADS—John Denver

156 TEACH YOUR CHILDREN—Crosby, Stills, Nash & Young

163 THIS LAND IS YOUR LAND—Woody & Arlo Guthrie

170 TIME IN A BOTTLE—Jim Croce

175 TURN! TURN! TURN! (To Everything There Is a Season)—The Byrds

181 UP ON THE ROOF—James Taylor

190 WE SHALL OVERCOME—Pete Seeger

192 WILD WORLD—Cat Stevens

196 YOU'RE ONLY LONELY—J.D. Souther

203 YOU'VE GOT A FRIEND—James Taylor

215 Guitar Notation Legend

ISBN 0-634-02377-2

HAL•LEONARD
CORPORATION

7777 W. BLUEMOUND RD. P.O.BOX 13819 MILWAUKEE, WI 53213

Visit Hal Leonard Online at
www.halleonard.com

At Seventeen

Words and Music by Janis Ian

*Sound of R.H. fingers hitting strings.

love   was meant for beau -   ty queens ___   and high ___ school girls ___
Fri - day night cha - rades ___ of youth ___   were spent ___ on one ___

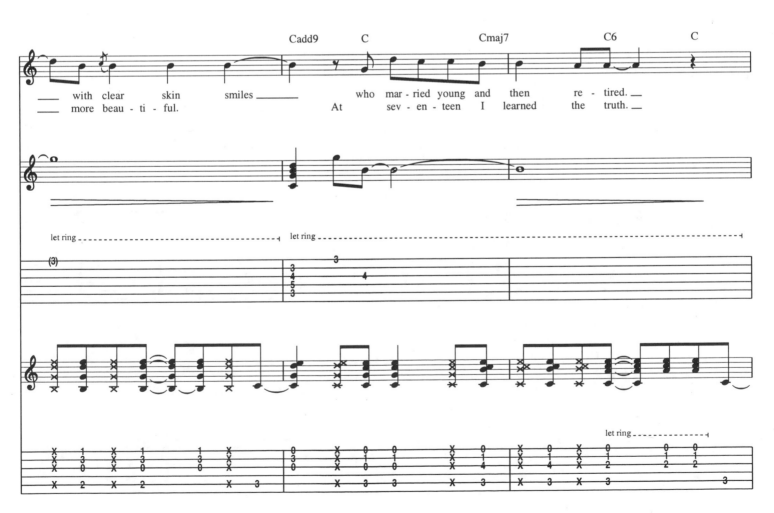

___ with clear skin smiles ___   who mar - ried young and then re - tired. ___
___ more beau - ti - ful.   At sev - en - teen I learned the truth. ___

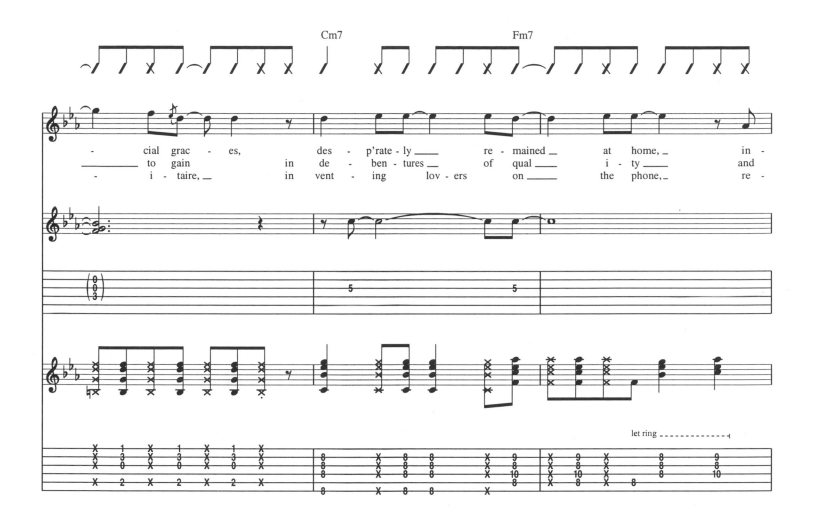

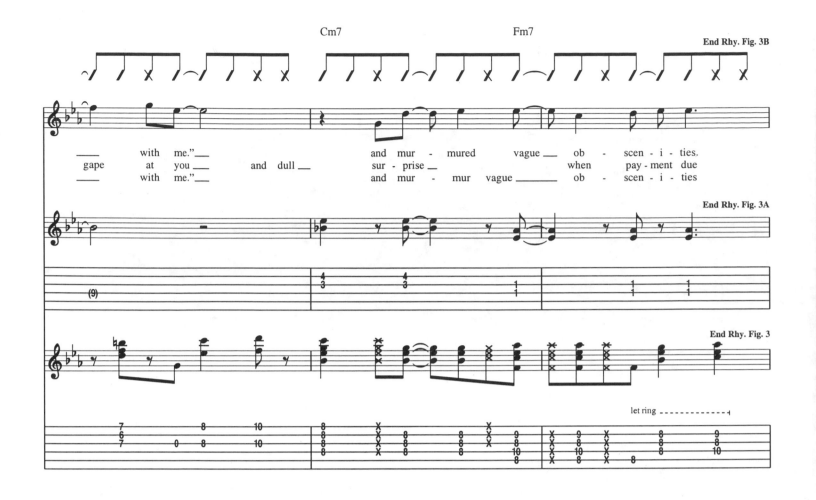

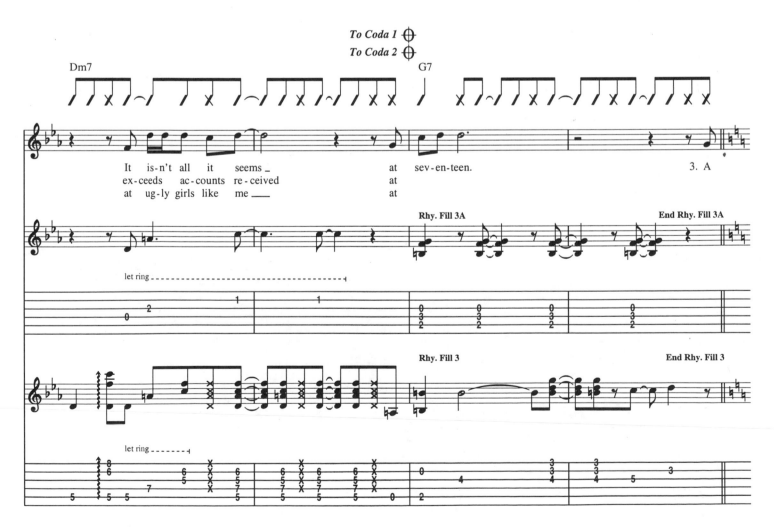

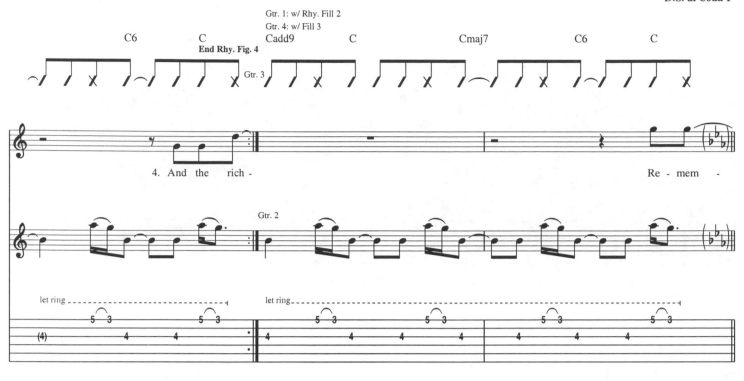

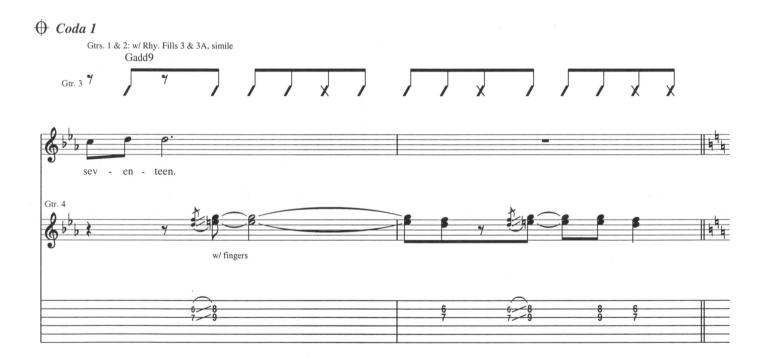

Interlude

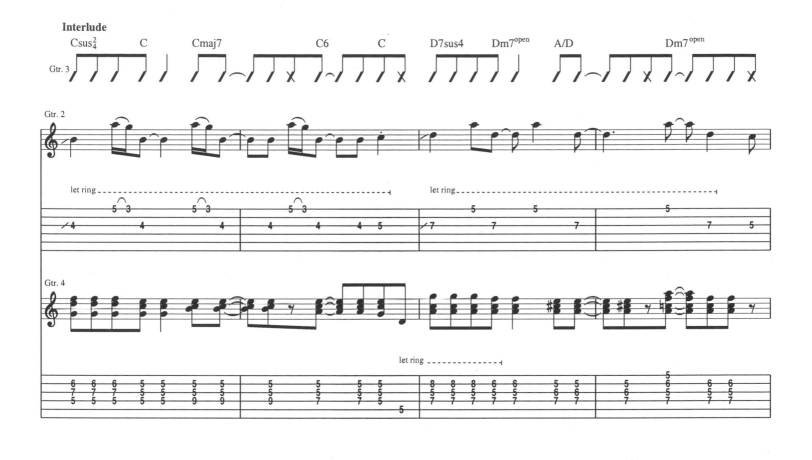

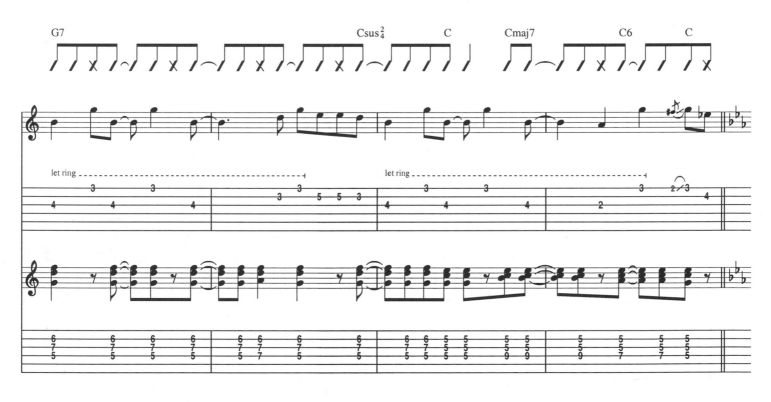

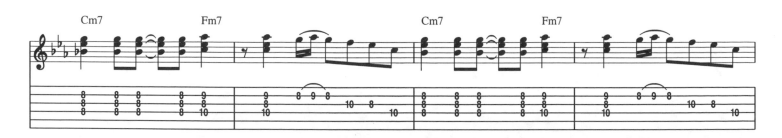

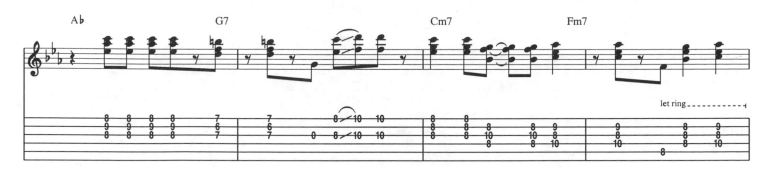

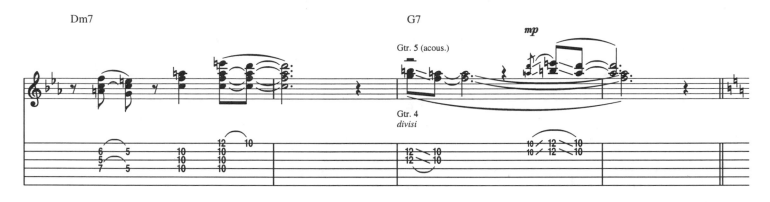

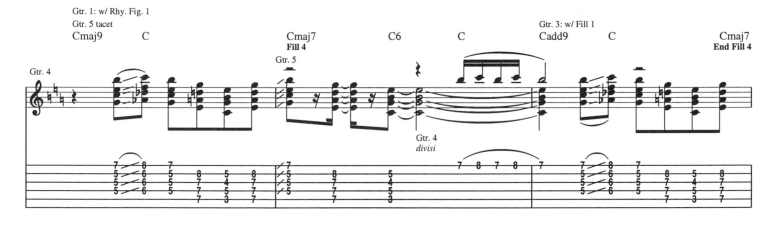

Verse

5. To those ___ of us who knew ___ the pain ___ of

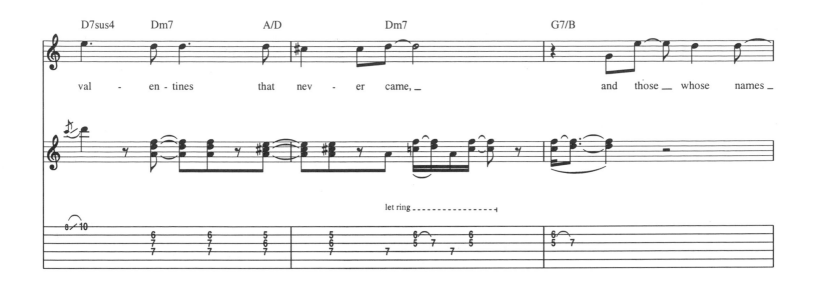

val - en - tines that nev - er came, ___ and those ___ whose names ___

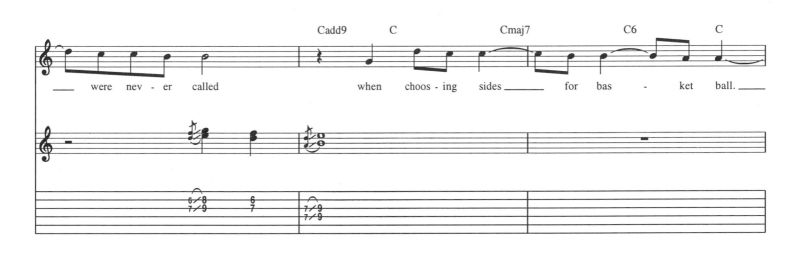

___ were nev - er called when choos - ing sides _____ for bas - ket ball. ___

Verse

Gtr. 1: w/ Rhy. Fig. 2, 1st 8 meas.
Gtr. 3: w/ Rhy. Fig. 4, simile

6. It was long ___ a - go ___ and far ___ a - way, ___

the world ___ was _ young - er than _ to-day, _ and dreams ___ were all _ they gave _ for free

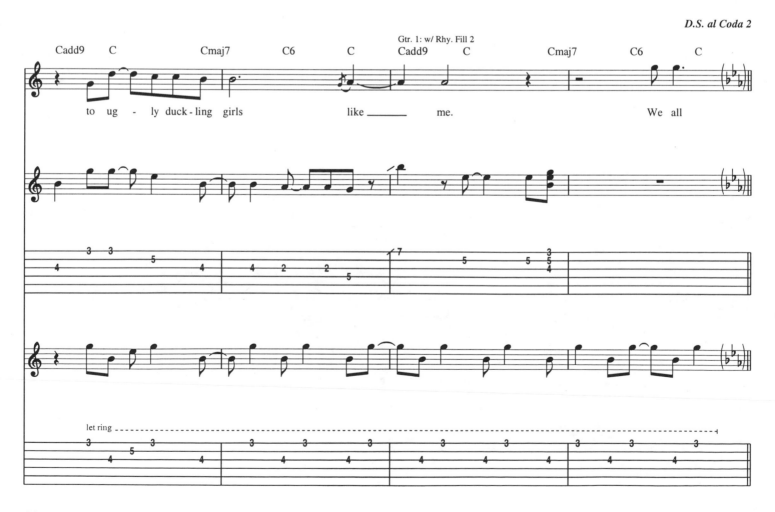

to ug - ly duck - ling girls like _____ me. We all

sev - en - teen.

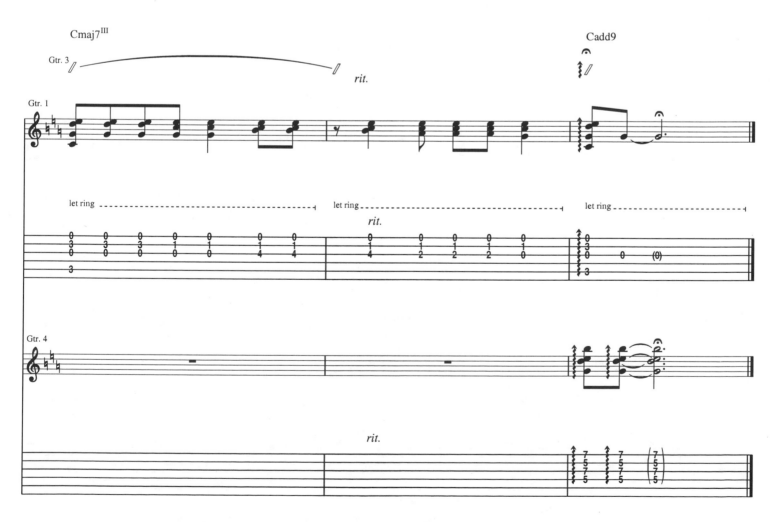

Best of My Love

Words and Music by John David Souther, Don Henley and Glenn Frey

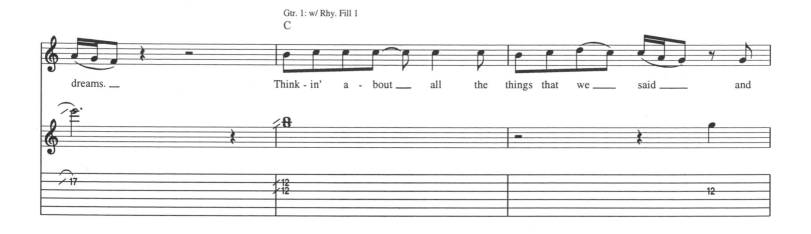

Gtr. 1: w/ Rhy. Fill 1

dreams. __ Think - in' a - bout __ all the things that we __ said __ and

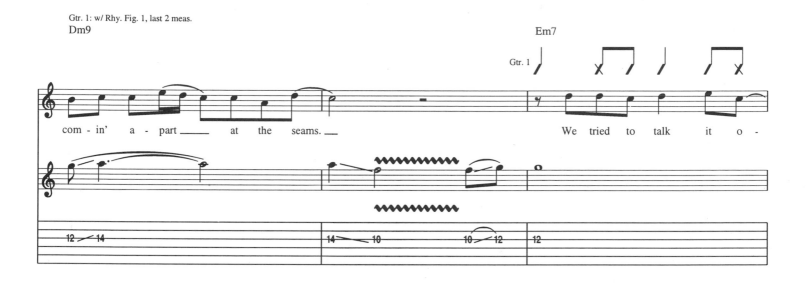

Gtr. 1: w/ Rhy. Fig. 1, last 2 meas.

com - in' a - part __ at the seams. __ We tried to talk it o -

(cont. in notation)

- ver __ but the words come out __ too __ rough. __ I

Rhy. Fill 1
Gtr. 1

let ring -

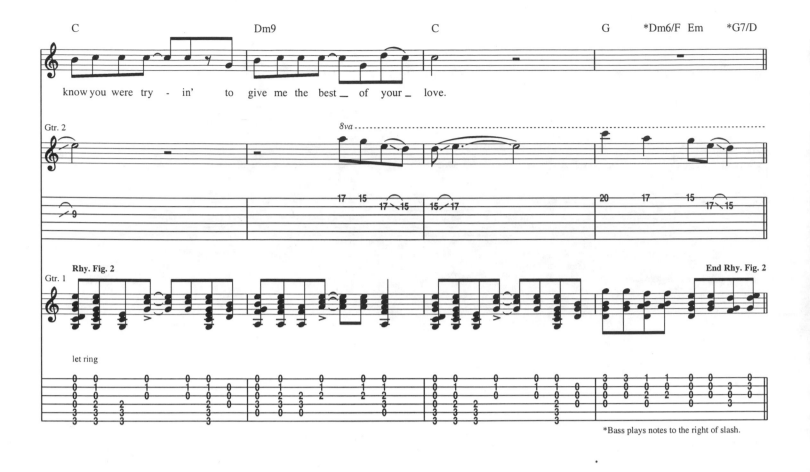

know you were try - in' to give me the best __ of your __ love.

Gtr. 2

8va

Rhy. Fig. 2

Gtr. 1

End Rhy. Fig. 2

let ring

*Bass plays notes to the right of slash.

Verse

Gtr. 1: w/ Rhy. Fig. 1, 2 times, simile

2. Beau - ti - ful fac - es and loud emp - ty plac - es, look at the way that we live. __

Gtr. 2 *8va*

loco

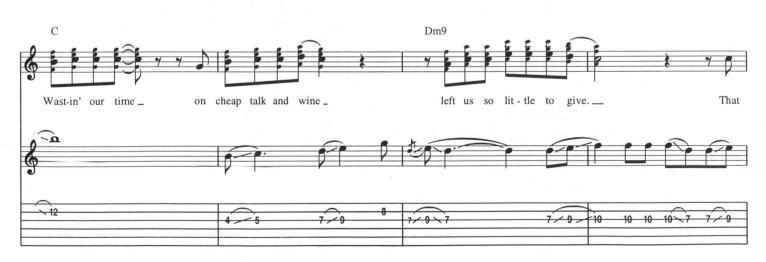

Wast-in' our time __ on cheap talk and wine __ left us so lit - tle to give. __ That

*F   Cmaj7

you get the best of my love. _____ Whoa, _____ sweet dar-
love.)

*Bass plays D.

F

End Rhy. Fig. 4

-lin',   you get the best of my ___ love.
(You get the best of my love. ___)

p   *mp*

Bridge

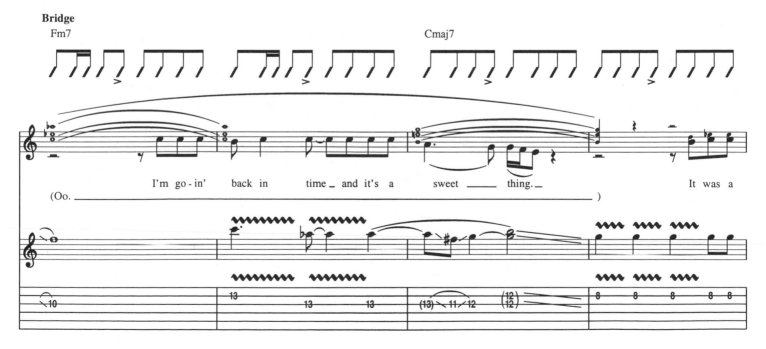

Fm7   Cmaj7

I'm go-in' back in time _ and it's a   sweet _____ thing. _   It was a
(Oo. _____)

*Fret higher note w/o slide

Verse

Gtr. 1: w/ Rhy. Fig. 1, 2 times, simile

Outro-Chorus

*Refers to downstemmed notes only.

Blackbird

Words and Music by John Lennon and Paul McCartney

*Strum upstemmed notes w/ index fin. of pick hand
whenever more than one upstemmed note appears.

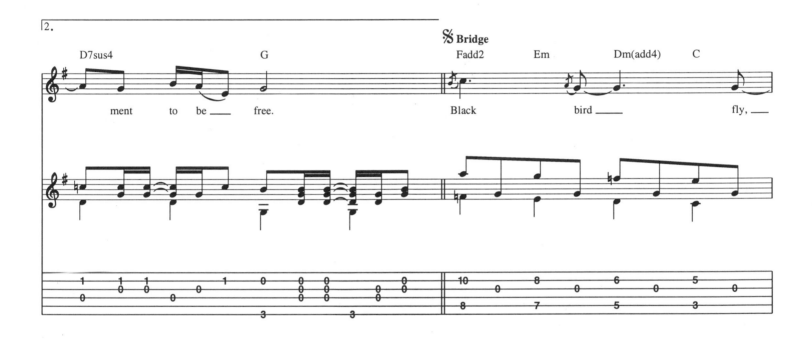

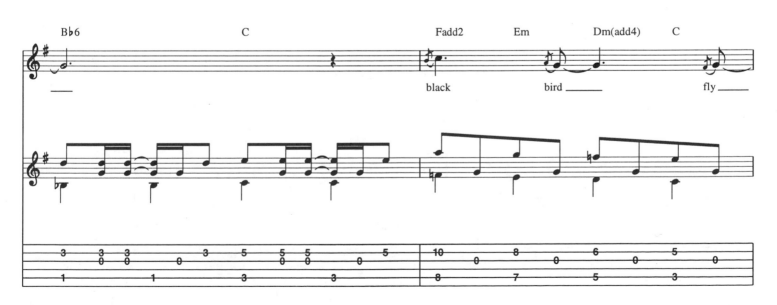

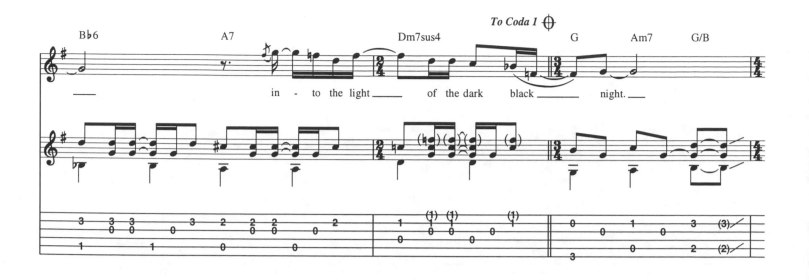

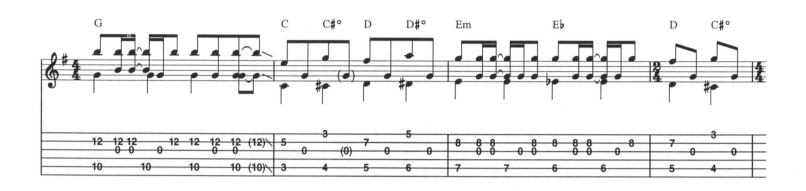

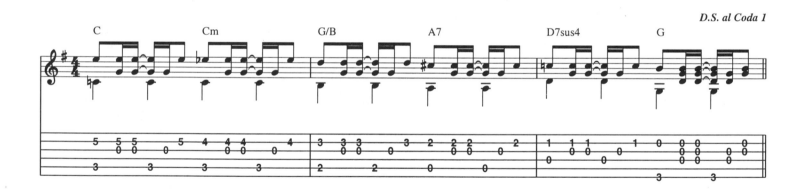

D.S. al Coda 1

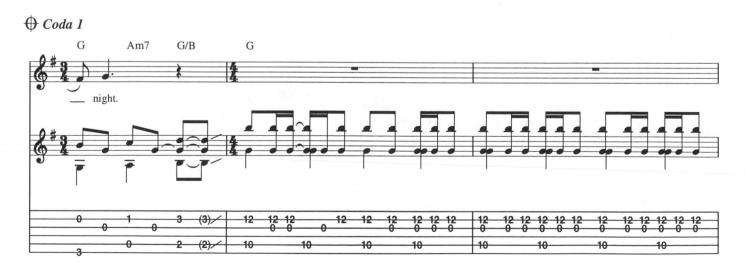

🔶 *Coda 2*

Chicago

Words and Music by Graham Nash

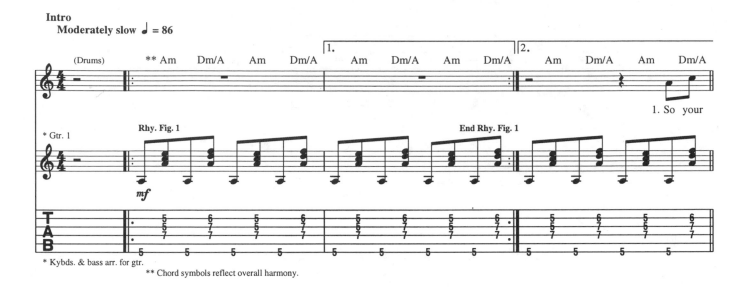

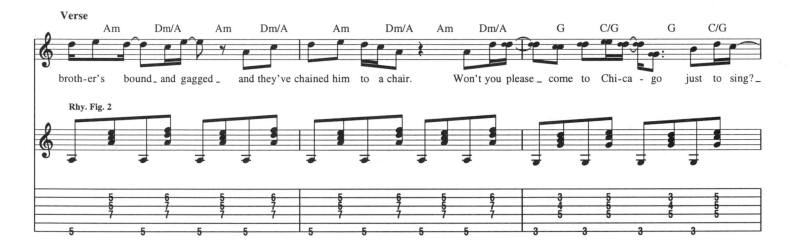

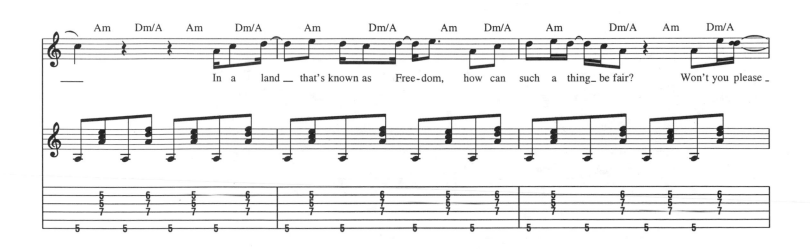

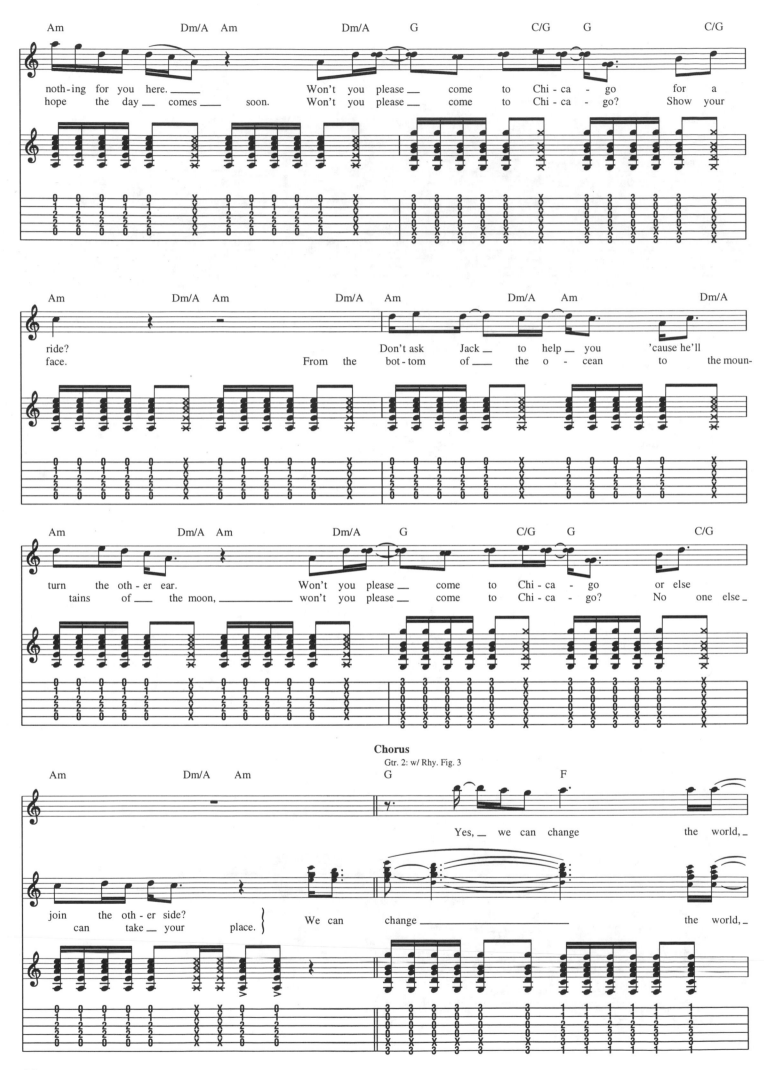

Chorus
Gtr. 2: w/ Rhy. Fig. 3

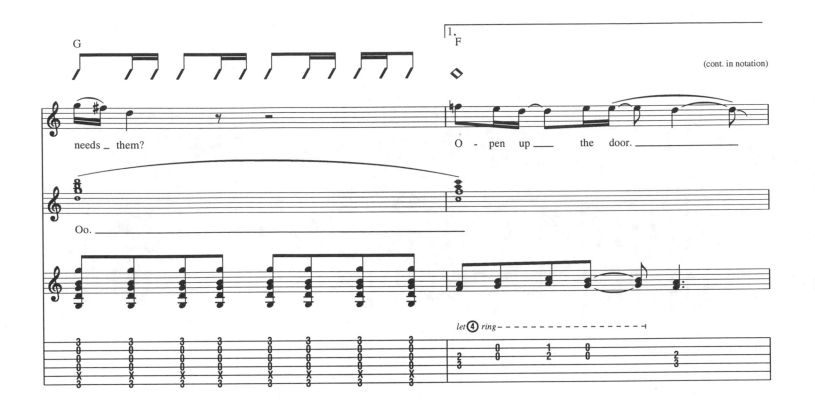

needs _ them?

Oo. _

O - pen up ___ the door. ___

(cont. in notation)

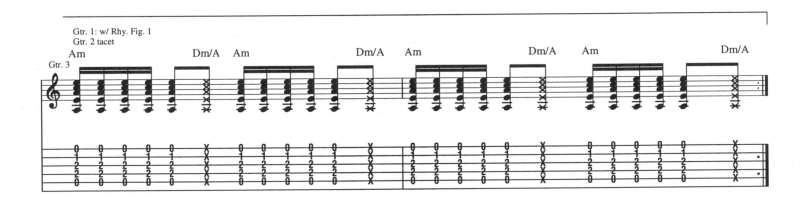

Gtr. 1: w/ Rhy. Fig. 1
Gtr. 2 tacet

Gtr. 3

Am   Dm/A Am   Dm/A Am   Dm/A Am   Dm/A

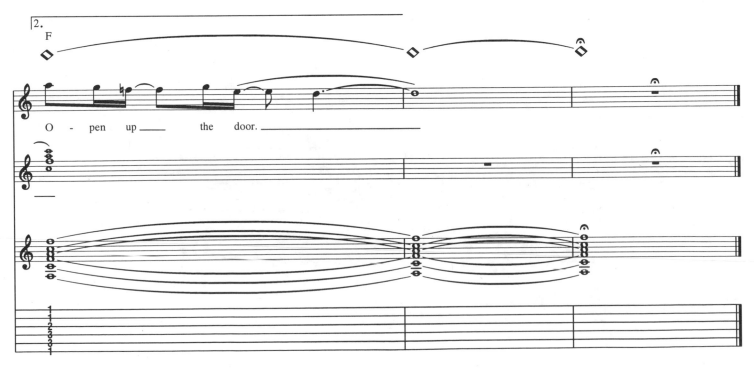

O - pen up ___ the door. ___

Crying

Words and Music by Roy Orbison and Joe Melson

* Piano arr. for gtr.

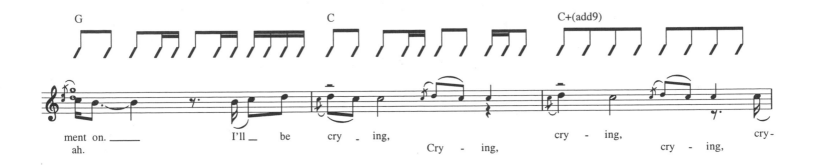

ment on. _____ I'll _ be cry - ing, cry - ing, cry -

ah.   Cry - ing,

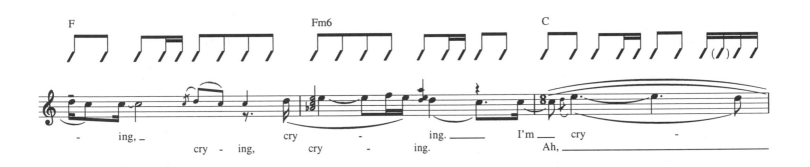

- ing, _   cry   -   ing. _____ I'm _ cry   -

cry - ing,   cry   -   ing.   Ah, _____

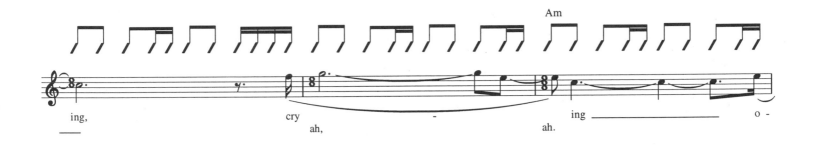

ing,   cry   -   ing _____   o -

ah,   ah.

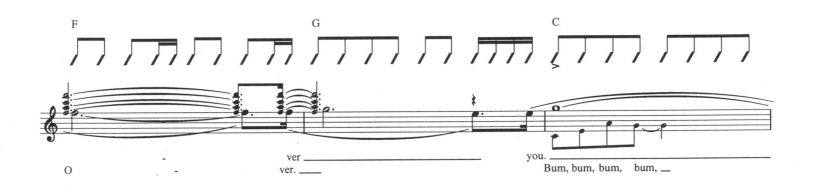

O   -   ver _____   you.

Bum, bum, bum,   bum, __

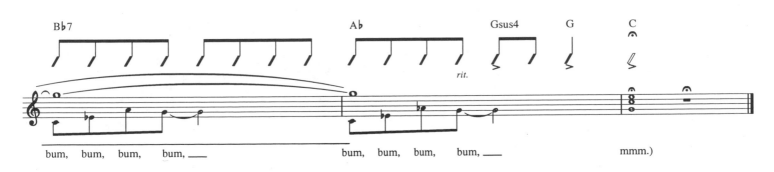

bum,   bum,   bum,   bum, _____   bum,   bum,   bum,   bum, _____   mmm.)

Dark Hollow

Words and Music by Bill Browning

Gtr. 2: Capo II

* Intro
Moderately slow, in 2 ♩ = 92

* Preceded by 32 seconds of talking, warming up, etc.
** Symbols in parentheses represent chord names respective to capoed guitar.
Symbols above reflect actual sounding chord. Capoed fret is "0" in tab.

Verse

Rhy. Fig. 1

let ring throughout

1. I'd rather be in some dark hol-ler where the

sun _____ don't _ ev - er shine _____ then to be _____

Rhy. Fig. 2

_____ home a - lone. _____ Know-ing that _ you're gone _____ would

cause me to lose my mind. ___ So

End Rhy. Fig. 2

P.M. ┙   P.M. ┙

End Rhy. Fig. 1

𝄋 Chorus

1st & 2nd times, Gtr. 2: w/ Rhy. Fig. 1
3rd time, Gtr. 2: w/ Rhy. Fig. 1 (1st 14 meas.)

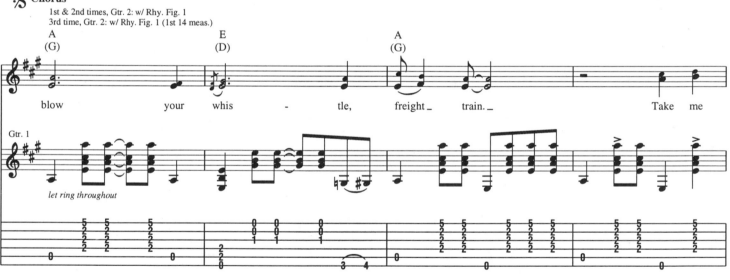

blow your whis - tle, freight ___ train. ___ Take me

Gtr. 1

let ring throughout

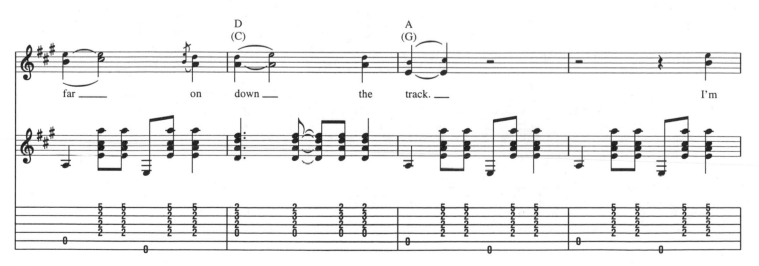

far ___ on down ___ the track. ___ I'm

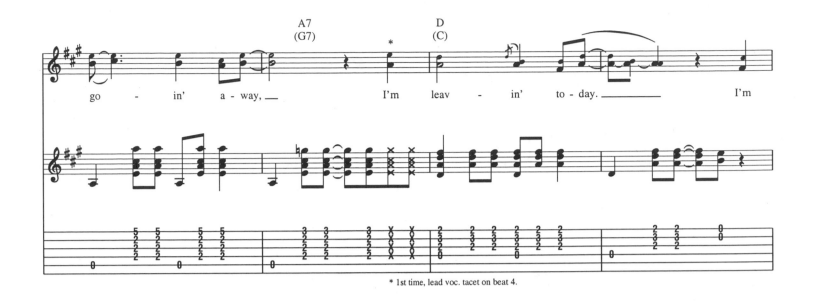

A7
(G7)

D
(C)

go - in' a - way, ___ I'm leav - in' to - day. ___ I'm

* 1st time, lead voc. tacet on beat 4.

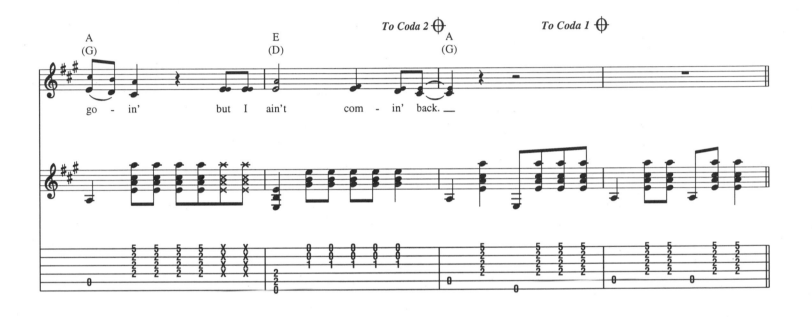

To Coda 2 ⊕

To Coda 1 ⊕

A
(G)

E
(D)

A
(G)

go - in'   but I ain't   com - in' back. ___

Guitar Solo

Gtr. 2

A
(G)

D
(C)

E
(D)

A
(G)

let ring throughout

Gtr. 1

let ring throughout

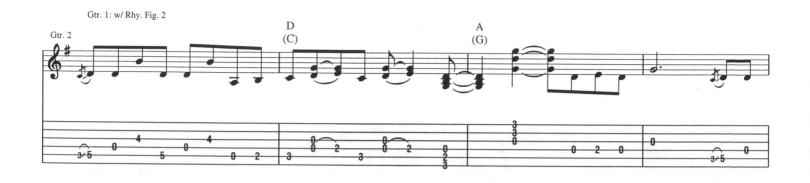

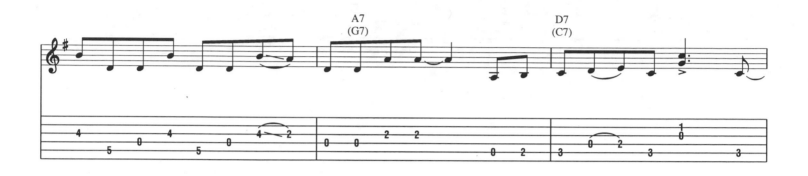

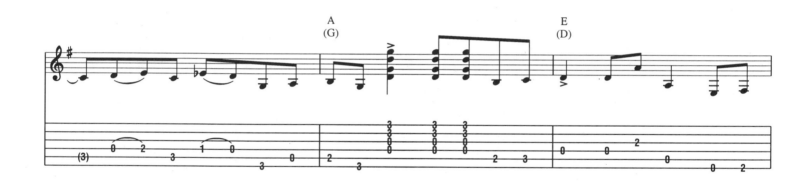

41

⊕ Coda 1

Guitar Solo
Gtr. 2: w/ Rhy. Fig. 1

* Catch 2nd string w/ L.H. ring finger.

D.S. al Coda 2

⊕ Coda 2

Do You Believe in Magic

Words and Music by John Sebastian

wipe off your face __ no mat- ter how hard you try. __ Your feet start tap- pin' and you

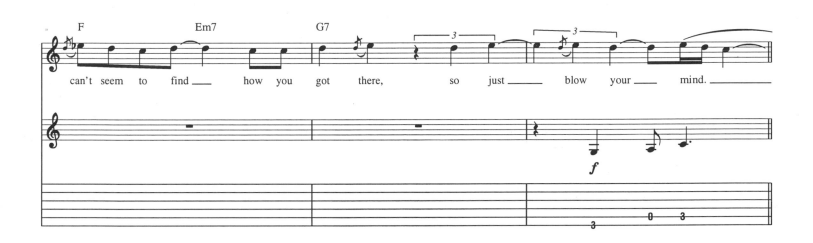

can't seem to find __ how you got there, so just __ blow your __ mind. __

Guitar Solo

Gtr. 1

Gtr. 2

Gtr. 1: w/ Rhy. Fig. 2

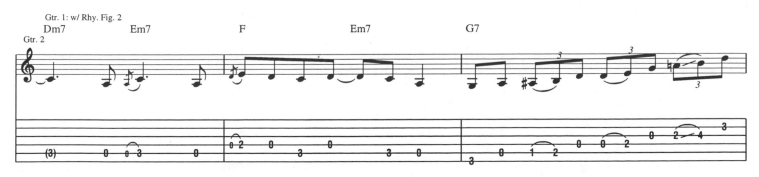

Gtr. 2

Verse

Gtr. 1: w/ Rhy. Fig. 1

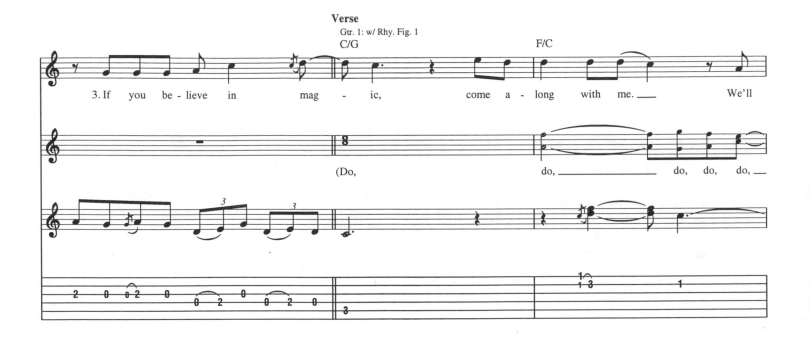

3. If you be-lieve in mag - ic, come a-long with me. ___ We'll

(Do, do, ___ do, do, do,

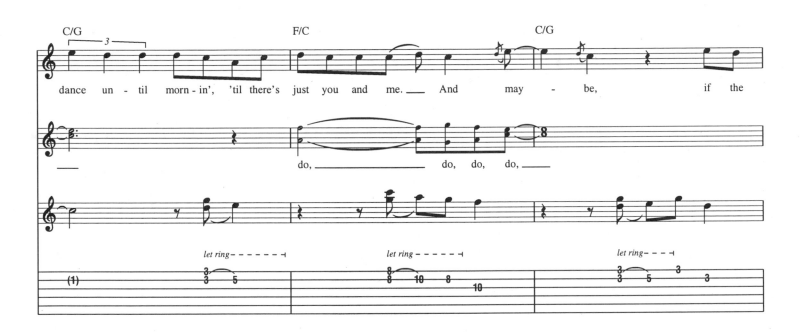

dance un - til morn - in', 'til there's just you and me. ___ And may - be, if the

do, ___ do, do, do, ___

let ring ------ let ring ------ let ring ----

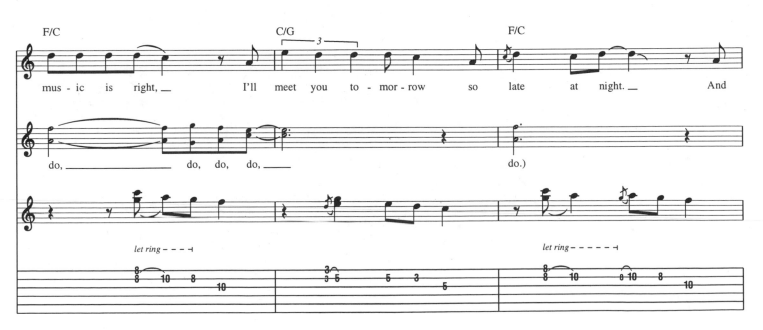

mus - ic is right, ___ I'll meet you to - mor - row so late at night. ___ And

do, ___ do, do, do, ___ do.)

let ring ---- let ring ------

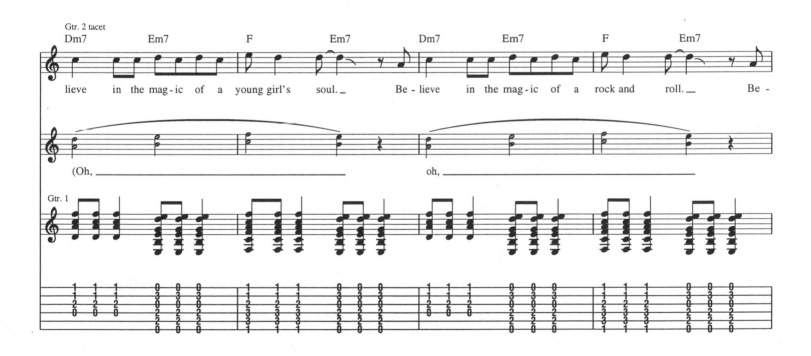

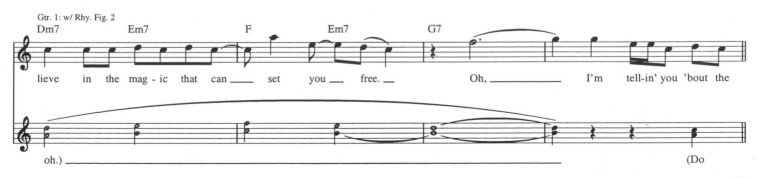

Outro

Gtr. 1: w/ Rhy. Fig. 3 (till fade)

Doctor, My Eyes

Words and Music by Jackson Browne

Gtr. 1: Capo I

Intro

Moderately ♩ = 152

* Gtr. 1

mf
w/ fingers
let ring throughout

* Piano arr. for gtr.   ** Symbols in parentheses reflect chord names respective to capoed guitar.
Symbols above reflect actual sounding chords. Capoed fret is "0" in tab.
Chord symbols reflect implied harmony.

Verse

Rhy. Fig. 1

1. Doc - tor, my ___ eyes have seen the years ___ and the slow ___

___ pa - rade ___ of fears _____ with - out cry - ing. Now I want ___

* T = Thumb on 6th string

51

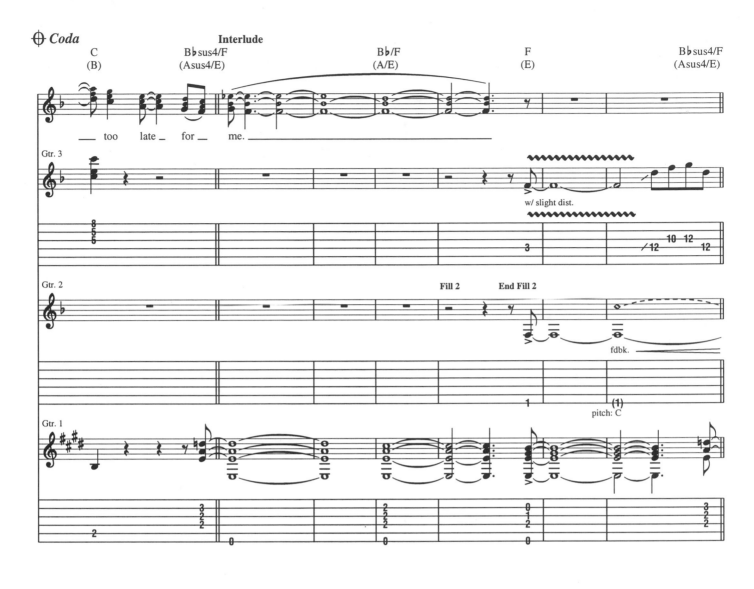

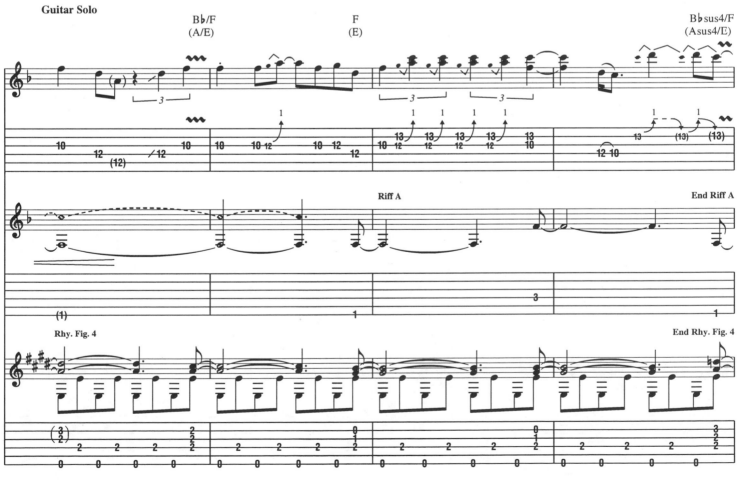

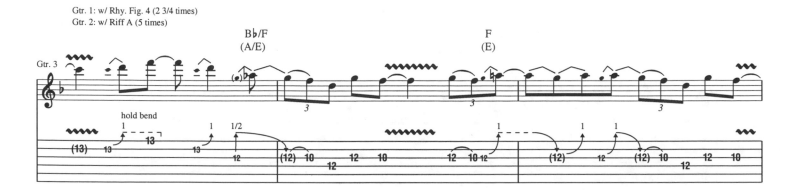

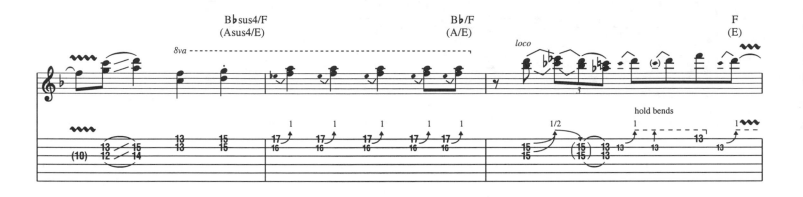

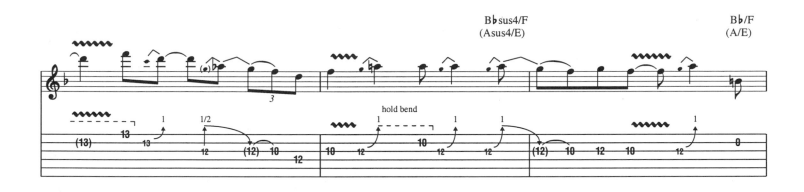

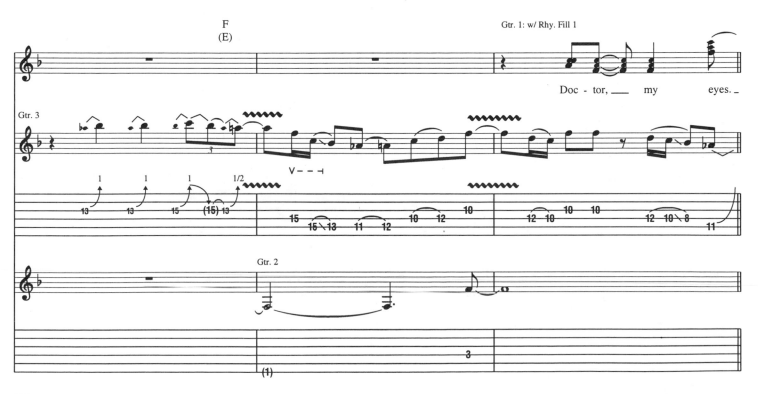

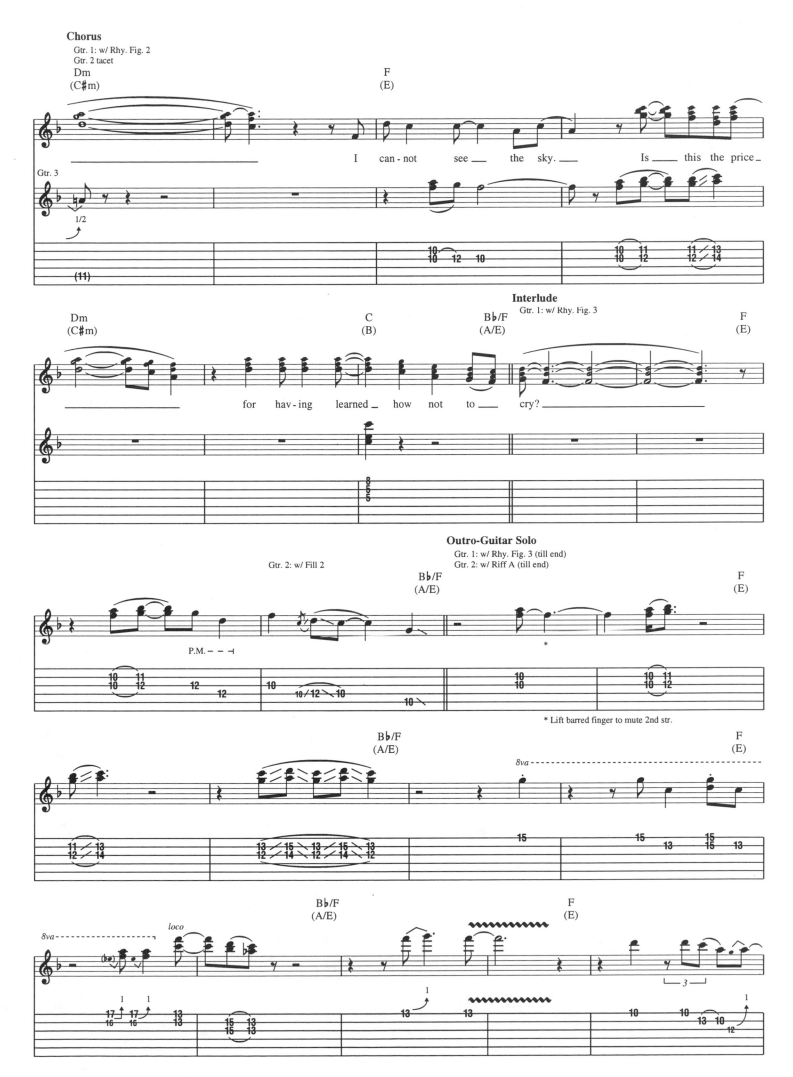

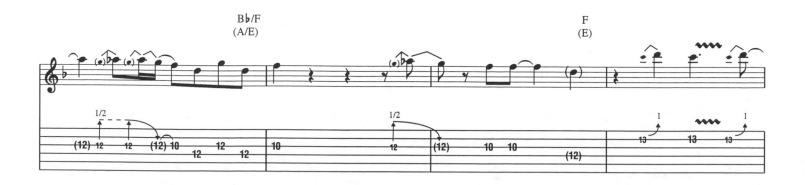

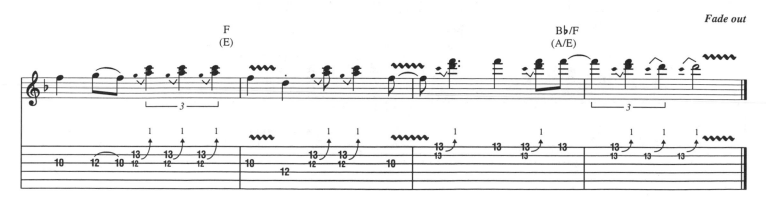

Eight Miles High

Words and Music by Roger McGuinn, David Crosby and Gene Clark

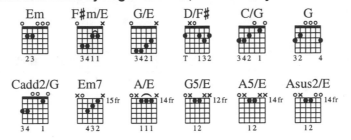

Verse

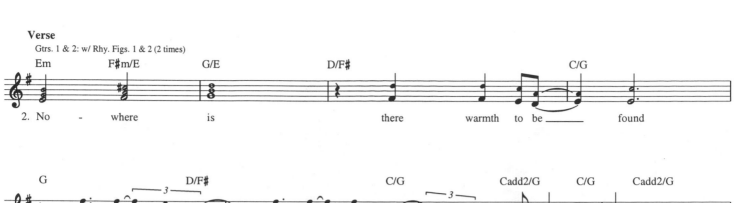

2. No - where is there warmth to be _____ found

a - mong _ those a - fraid of _ los - ing _____ their _ ground. _____

Rain - grey town known for its _____ sound,

in plac - es _____ small fac - es un - bound. _____

Guitar Solo

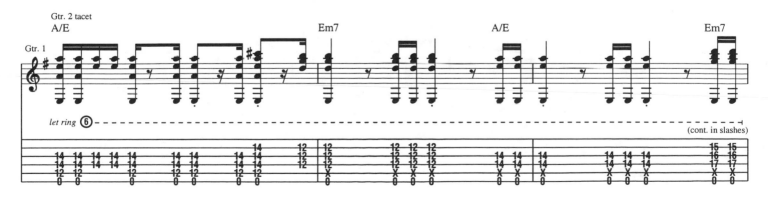

and black lim-o - sines,   some liv-ing, ___   some stand-ing a - lone. ___

Outro

Gtr. 2: w/ Rhy. Fig. 3

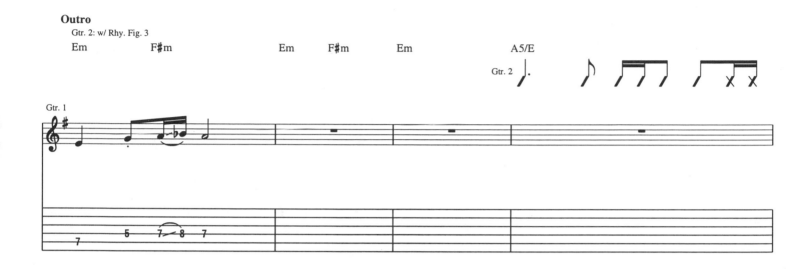

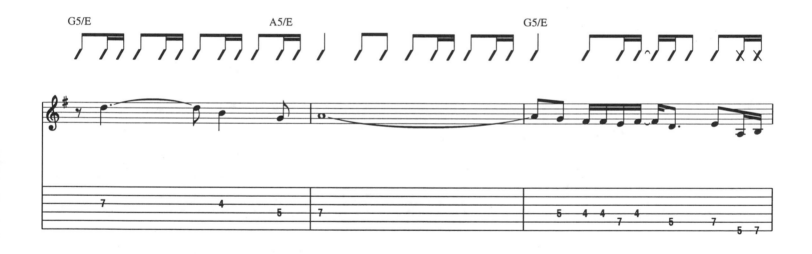

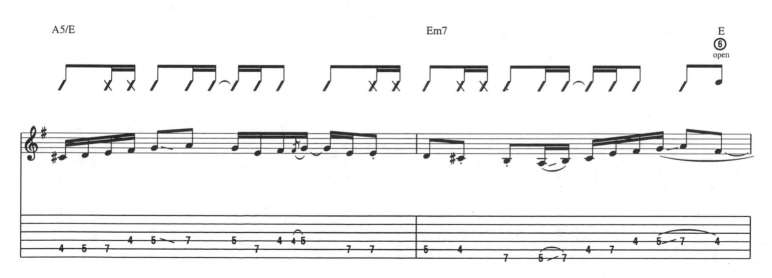

Fire and Rain

Words and Music by James Taylor

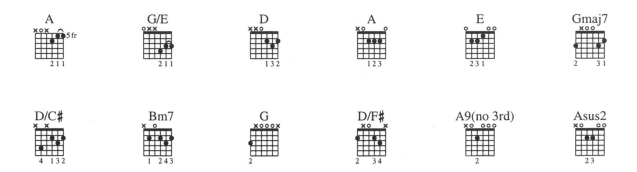

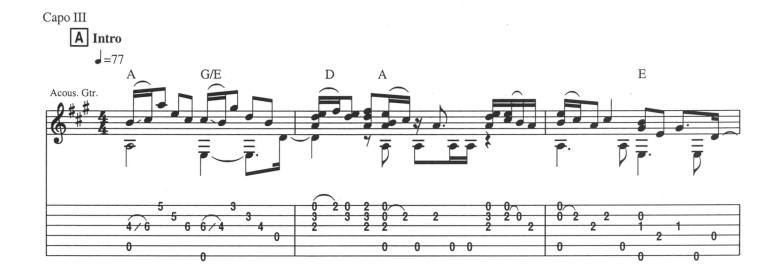

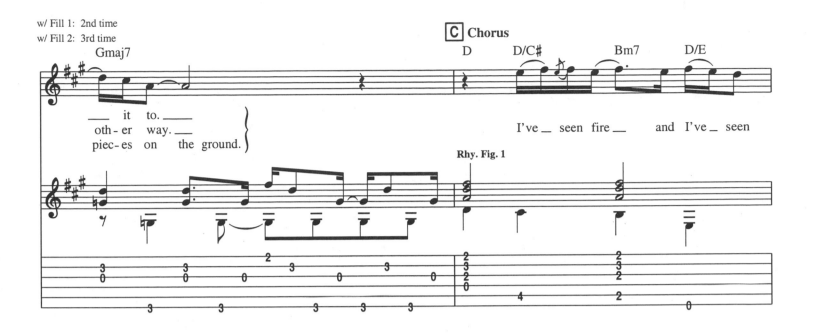

D Outro

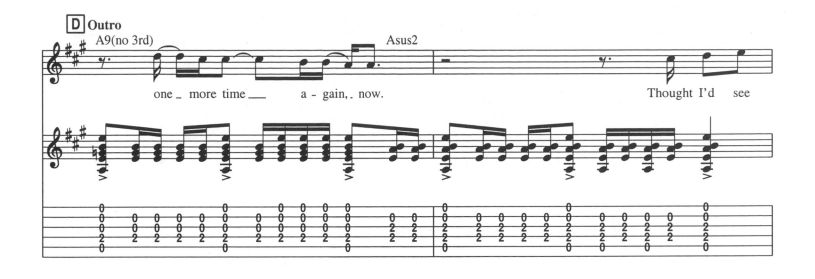

one _ more time ___ a - gain, now.   Thought I'd   see

Strumming simile

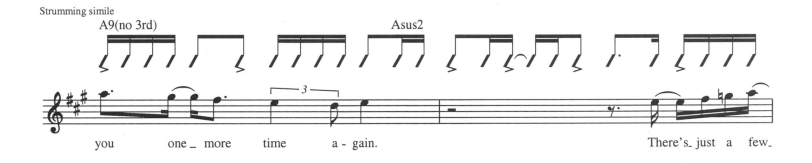

you   one _ more   time   a - gain.   There's_ just a few_

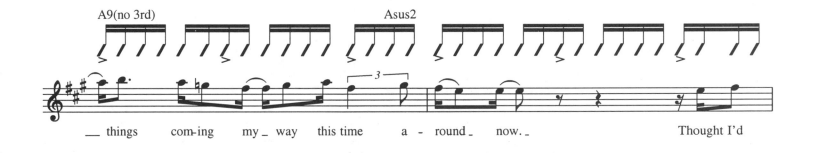

_ things   com-ing   my _   way   this time   a - round_   now. _   Thought I'd

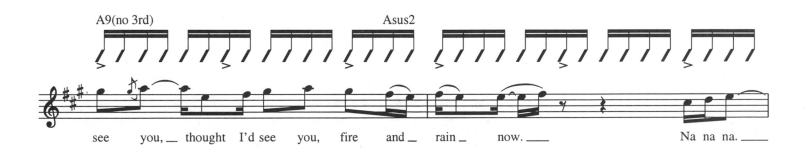

see   you, __ thought   I'd   see   you,   fire   and _   rain _   now. ___   Na   na   na. ____

Fade

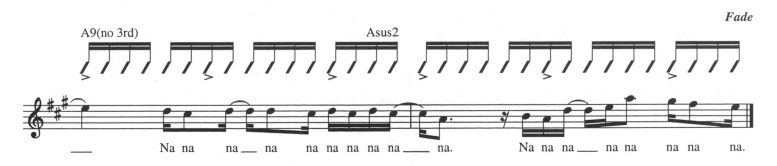

_   Na   na   na _   na   na   na   na   na   na. ___   na.   Na   na   na ___   na   na   na   na   na.

69

Happy Together

Words and Music by Garry Bonner and Alan Gordon

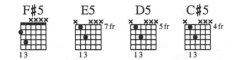

* Chord symbols reflect baisc harmony.

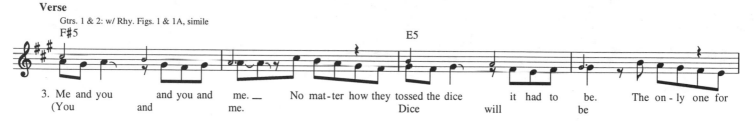

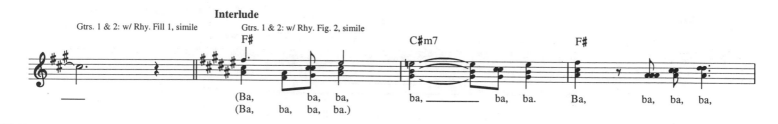

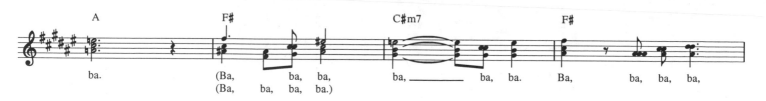

72

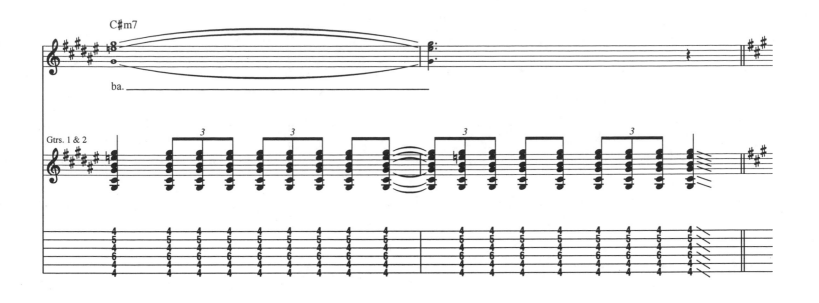

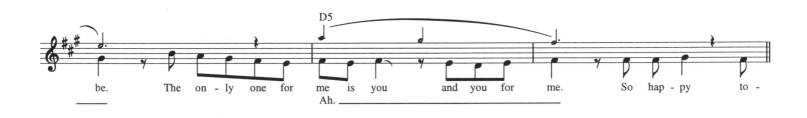

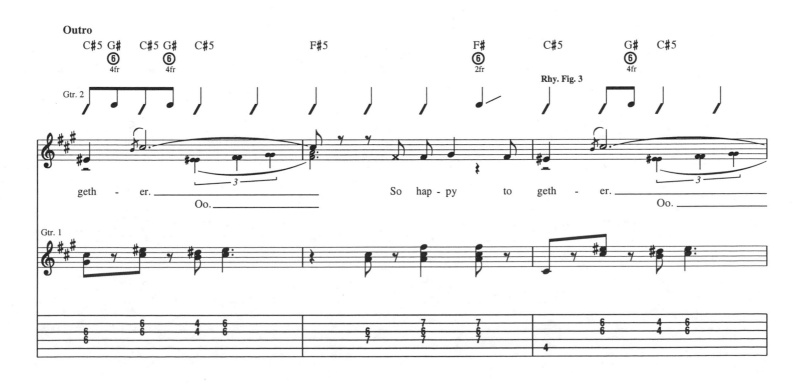

Help Me Make It Through the Night

Words and Music by Kris Kristofferson

Gtrs. 2 & 3; Tune Down Whole Step:

① = D ④ = C
② = A ⑤ = G
③ = F ⑥ = D

Gtr. 4; Open G Tuning:

① = D ④ = D
② = B ⑤ = G
③ = G ⑥ = D

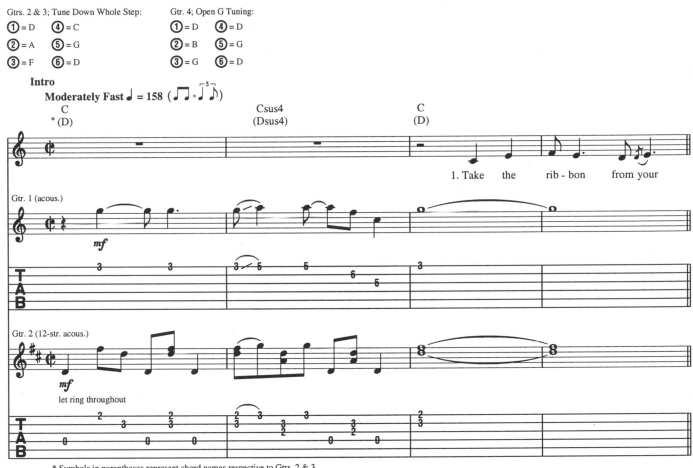

* Symbols in parentheses represent chord names respective to Gtrs. 2 & 3.
Symbols above reflect actual sounding chords.

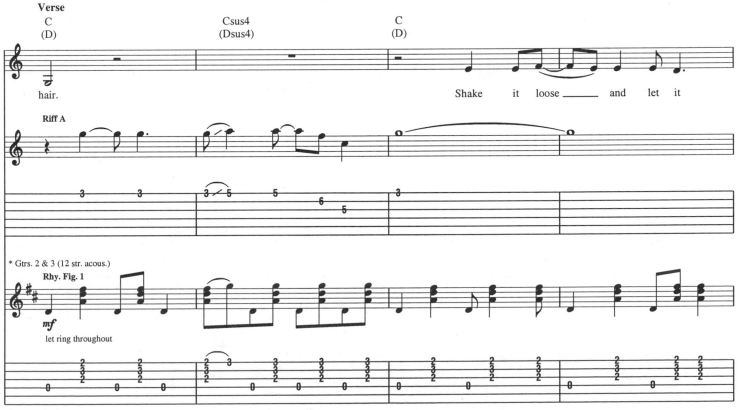

* composite arrangement

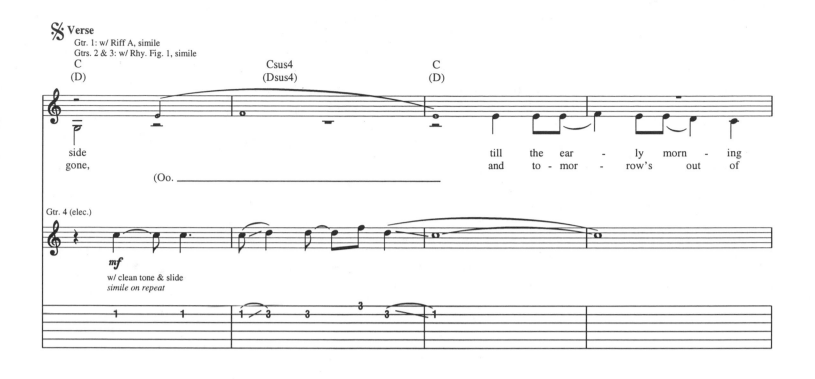

Gtr. 1: w/ Riff A, simile
Gtrs. 2 & 3: w/ Rhy. Fig. 1, simile

C
(D)

Csus4
(Dsus4)

C
(D)

side
gone,

(Oo. _____

till the ear - ly morn - ing
and to - mor - row's out of

Gtr. 4 (elec.)

mf

w/ clean tone & slide
simile on repeat

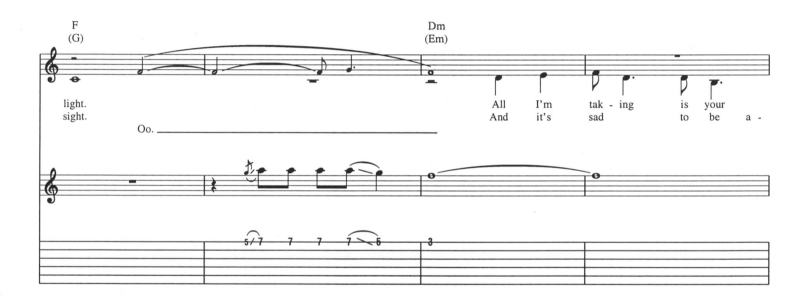

F
(G)

Dm
(Em)

light.
sight.

Oo. _____

All I'm tak - ing is your
And it's sad to be a -

G7   G7sus4   G7   G7sus4   G7
(A7)   (A7sus4)   (A7)   (A7sus4) (A7)

time. ___
lone. ___

Oo. _____

Help me make ___ it through the night. ___
Help me make ___ it through the night. ___

78

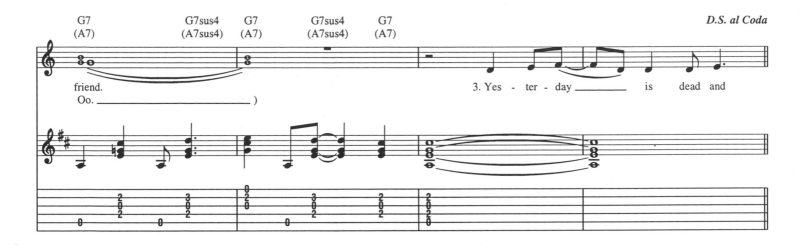

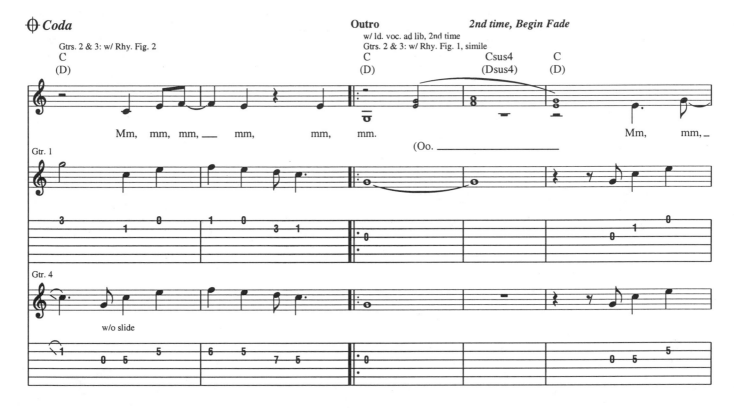

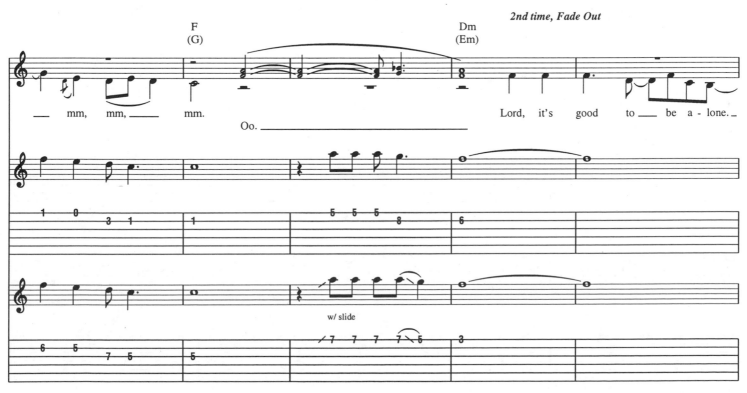

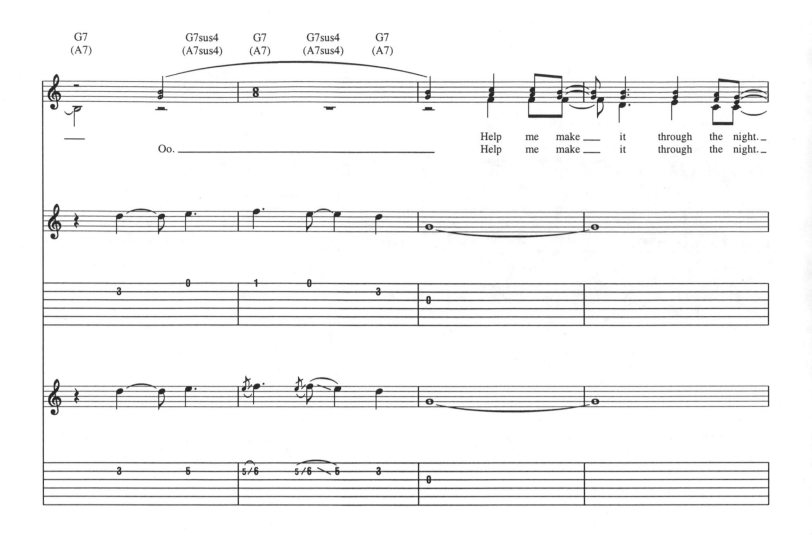

Help me make ___ it through the night. __
Help me make ___ it through the night. __

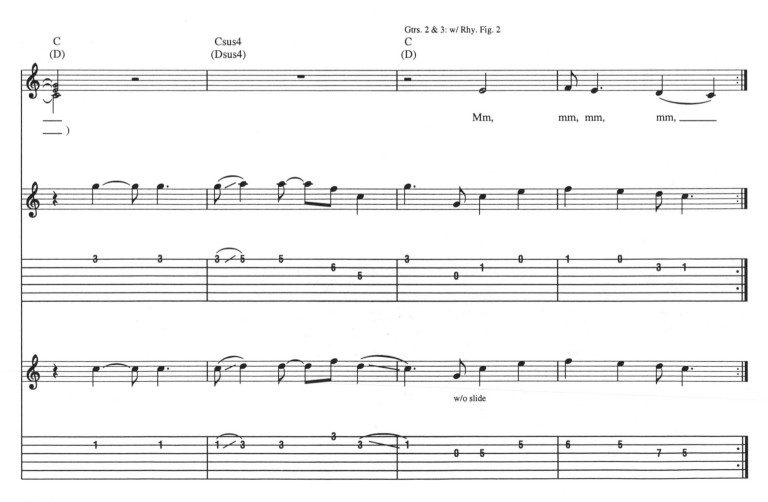

Gtrs. 2 & 3: w/ Rhy. Fig. 2

Mm,   mm, mm,   mm, ___

w/o slide

Here Comes the Sun

Words and Music by George Harrison

*Capo VII

Intro
Moderately ♩ = 126

Gtr. 1 (acous.)

*All notes tabbed on 7th fret are played as open strings

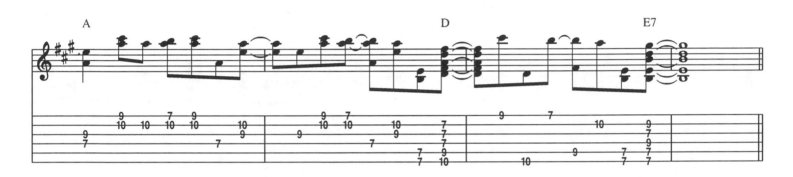

Chorus

Here comes _ the sun, ___ doo 'n' doo doo. Here comes _ the sun _

_ 'n' I _ say _ it's al - right.

Verse

1. Lit - tle dar - lin', it's ___ been ___ a ___ long, ___ cold, ___ lone - ly win - ter.

Lit - tle dar - lin', it ___ feels ___ like ___ years ___ since it's ___ been ___ here. ___

Chorus

Here comes ___ the sun, ___ doo 'n' doo doo. Here ___ comes ___ the sun ___ 'n' I ___ say

it's al - right.

Bridge

Sun, sun, sun, here it comes.

Sun, sun, sun, here it comes.

Verse

3. Lit-tle dar-lin', I ___ feel ___ that ___ ice ___ is ___ slow-ly ___ melt ___ ing.

84

If I Had a Hammer
(The Hammer Song)

Words and Music by Lee Hays and Pete Seeger

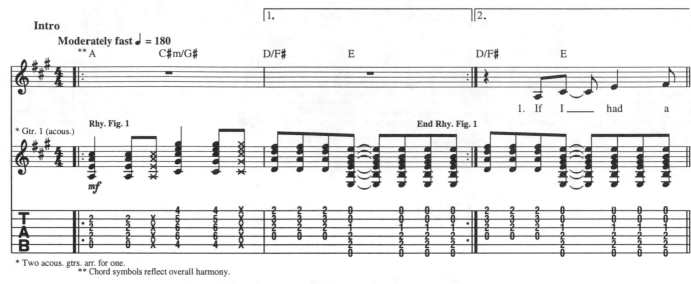

* Two acous. gtrs. arr. for one.
** Chord symbols reflect overall harmony.

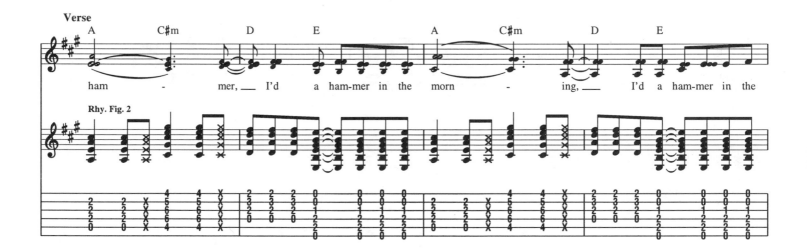

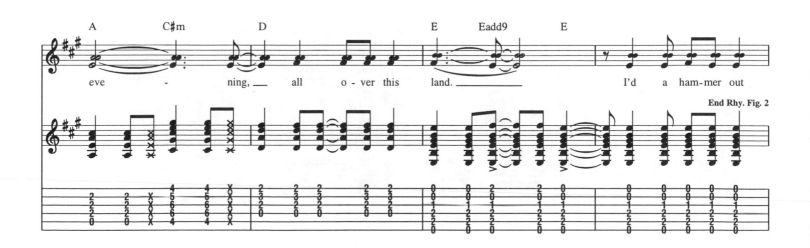

Just a Song Before I Go

Words and Music by Graham Nash

Gtrs. 3, 5 & 6: Capo II

Intro

Moderately ♩ = 112

* Elec. piano arr. for gtr.

Verse

Gtr. 1: w/ Rhy. Fig. 1 (2 times)
1st time, Gtr. 2 tacet
2nd time, Gtr. 2: w/ Fill 1
2nd time, Gtr. 5 tacet

1. Just a song _ be-fore _ I go _ to whom it may _ con- cern. _
   helped me with _ my suit- case, she stands be- fore _ my eyes. _

Gtr. 3 (acous.)

* Symbols in parentheses represent chord names respective to capoed guitar.
  Symbols above reflect actual sounding chord. Capoed fret is "0" in tab.

2. She _____ in love, _____ and she was gone.

Guitar Solo

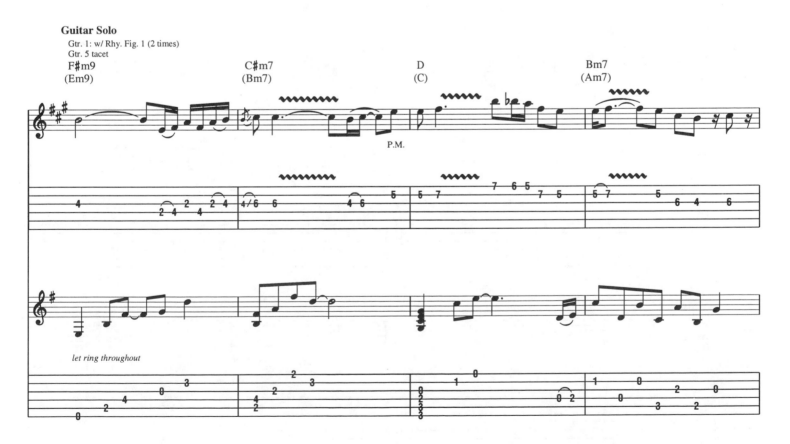

Gtr. 3: w/ Rhy. Fig. 2

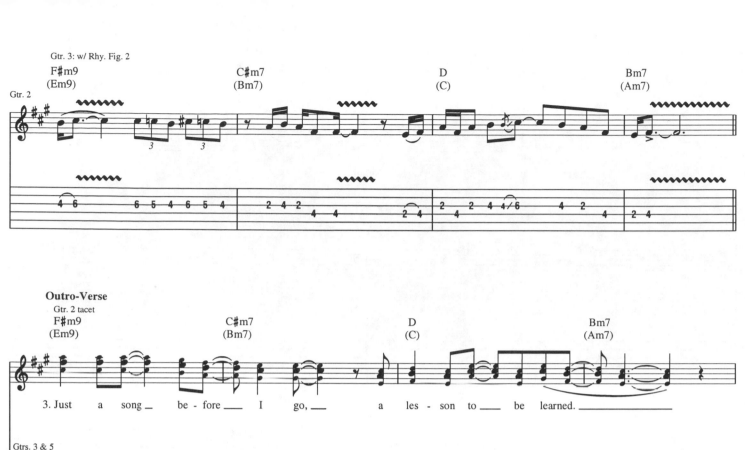

Outro-Verse

3. Just a song before I go, a les-son to be learned.

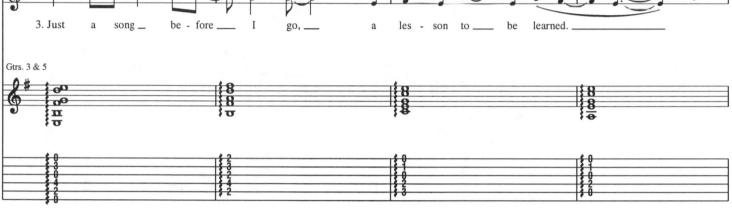

Trav-el-ing twice the speed of sound, it's eas-y to get burned.

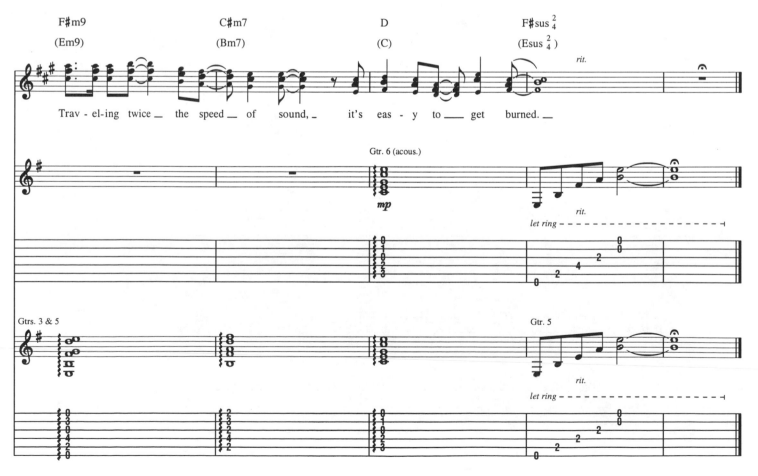

Last Night I Had the Strangest Dream

Words and Music by Ed McCurdy

*Banjo arr. for gtr.   **Chord symbols reflect basic harmony.

night   I _____ had   the _____ strang - est _____ dream   I
when   the _____ pa - pers   all   were _____ signed,   and a

*Revised first verse lyrics by Ed McCurdy.

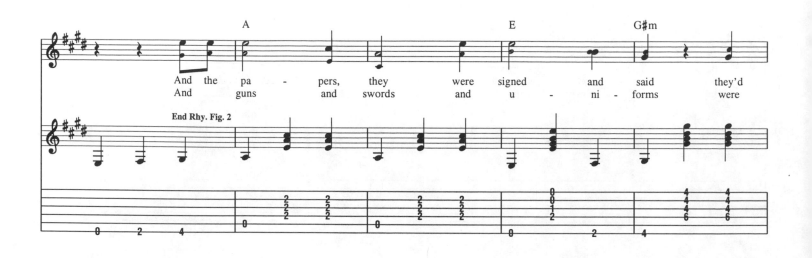

And the pa - pers, they were signed and said they'd
And guns and swords were and u - ni - forms were

nev - er ___ fight a - gain.
scat - tered ___ on the ground.

1.

2.

2. And

Banjo Solo

Gtr. 2: w/ Rhy. Fig. 2 (1st 3 meas.)

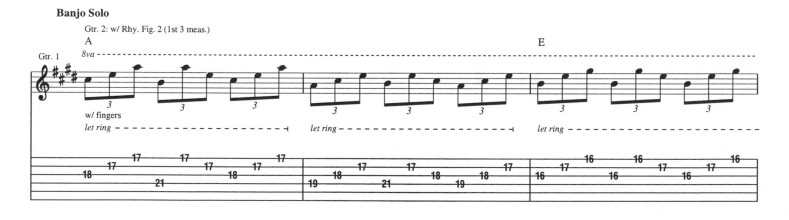

Gtr. 2: w/ Rhy. Fig. 2 (last meas.)

Gtr. 2: w/ Rhy. Fig. 2 (last 4 meas.)

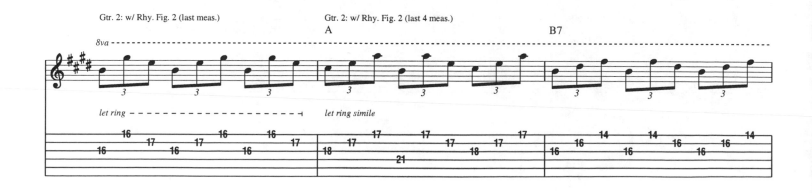

Gtr. 2: w/ Rhy. Fig. 2 (1st 2 meas.)

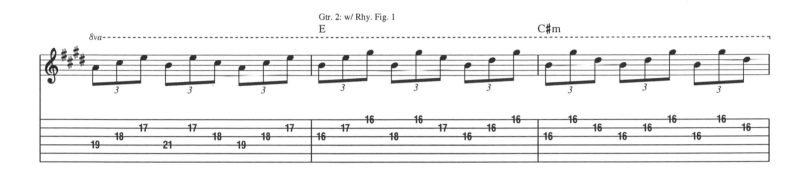

Gtr. 2: w/ Rhy. Fig. 1

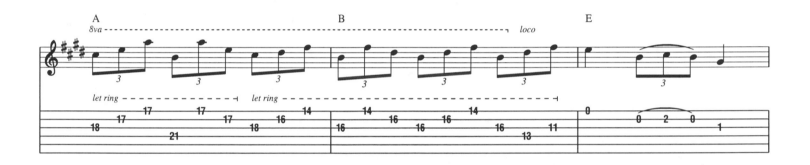

Coda

D.S. al Coda
(take 1st lyrics)

3. Last

Leader of the Band

Words and Music by Dan Fogelberg

*Symbols in parentheses represent chord names respective to capoed gtr. Symbols above reflect actual sounding chord. Capoed fret is "0" in TAB.
**Chord symbols reflect implied tonality.

1. An on-ly child a-lone and wild, a cab-'net mak-er's son,
2. A qui-et man of mu-sic de-nied a sim-pler fate,
3. My broth-ers' lives were dif-f'rent for they heard an-oth-er call.
4. I thank you for the mu-sic and your sto-ries of the

*omit 4th time

100

to im-i-tate the man. ___ I'm just a liv-ing leg-

To Coda 2

-a-cy to the lead - er of ___ the band.

D.S. al Coda 1

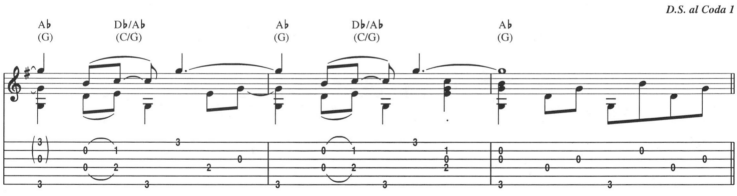

✛ *Coda 1*

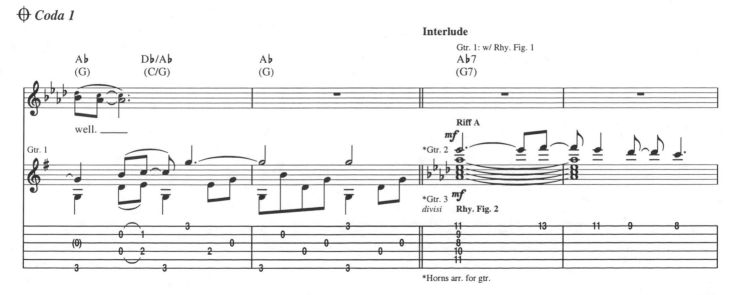

well. ___

Interlude

Gtr. 1: w/ Rhy. Fig. 1

Riff A

*Gtr. 2

Gtr. 1

*Gtr. 3
divisi **Rhy. Fig. 2**

*Horns arr. for gtr.

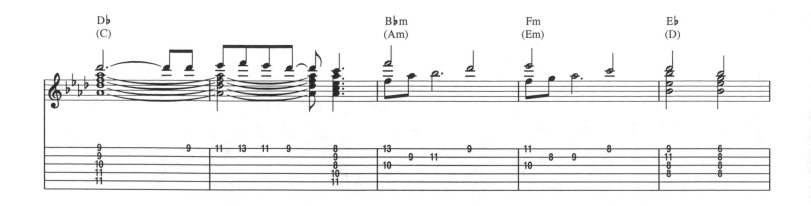

D.S. al Coda 2
(take 2nd ending)

End Riff A

End Rhy. Fig. 2

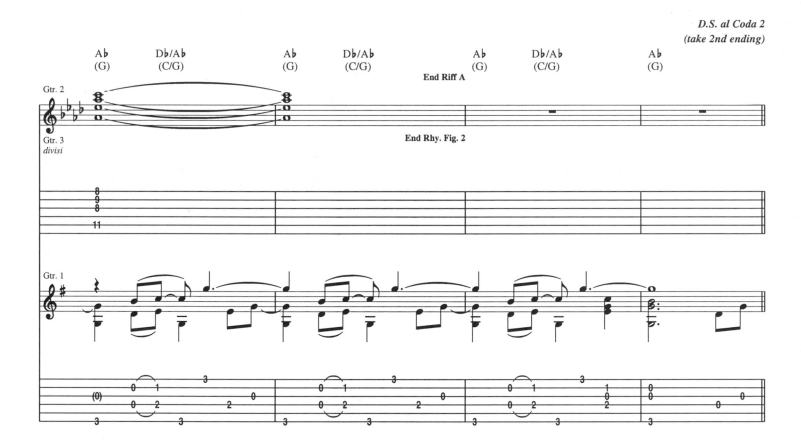

Coda 2

band.   I   am   the   liv - ing ____ leg - a - cy   to   the

lead - er   of _____ the band. _____

Outro

Gtrs. 2 & 3: w/ Riff A & Rhy. Fig. 2

Leaving on a Jet Plane

Words and Music by John Denver

sing for you. ___ When I come back ___ I'll wear your ___ wed - ding ring. ___ So

___ Oo. ___

___ Ah. ___ I'll wear your ___ ring. ___ So

Pre-Chorus

Gtr. 1: w/ Rhy. Fig. 2

A   D   A   D

kiss me and smile for me. ___ Tell me that ___ you'll wait for me. ___

A   Bm   E

Hold me like ___ you'll nev - er ___ let me go. ___ I'm a

(I'm)

Chorus

Gtr. 1: w/ Rhy. Fig. 3, simile

A   D   A   E   Esus4 D

leav - in' on a jet ___ plane. I don't know when I'll be back ___ a - gain. ___

A   C#m   Bm   E

___ Oh babe, ___ I ___ hate to go.

Verse

Gtr. 1: w/ Rhy. Fig. 1, 2 times

Amaj7   D6   Amaj7   D6

3. Now the time ___ has come to leave _ you. One more time, _ let me kiss _ you.

(Oo. ___

Amaj7   F#m   E   E7

Then close _ your eyes, ___ I'll be on my way. ___

Oo. ___ Oo. ___

Amaj7   D6   Amaj7   D6

Dream a - bout ___ the days to come _ when I won't have _ to leave a - lone, ___ a -

106

bout the time _____ I won't ____ have   to say: _____

Ah. _____ I ____ won't have ____ to say: __)

Pre-Chorus

*Gtr. 1: w/ Rhy. Fig. 2

Kiss   me and smile for me. ___   Tell me that _ you'll   wait   for me. ___

*grad. cresc. next 8 meas.

Hold   me like ___ you'll   nev - er _____ let me go. _____   I'm a
(I'm)

Outro-Chorus

Gtr. 1

*bass plays A this meas.

leav - in'   on   a jet __ plane.   I don't know when   I'll be back _ a - gain.

Leav - in   on   a jet ___ plane.   I don't   know   when
(Leav - in'

*D

*bass plays A

I'll   be back __ a - gain.   Leav -   in'   on   a jet ___ plane.
on   a jet ___ plane.   I don't   know when   I'll   be back __ a - gain. _____

*bass plays A

I don't   know when   I'll be back _ a - gain.   Oh babe, __   I hate _

_____)

*bass plays A

_____   to go. _____

Me and Bobby McGee

Words and Music by Kris Kristofferson and Fred Foster

* Quickly alternate between notes.

111

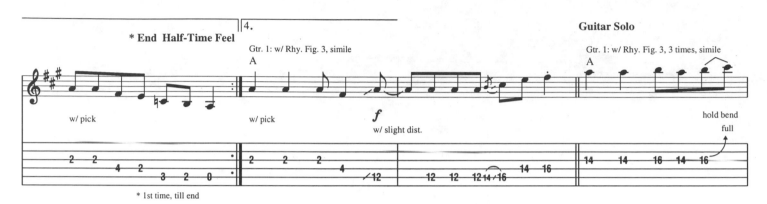

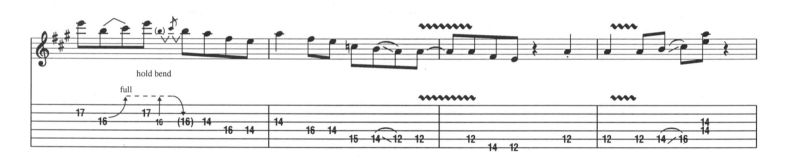

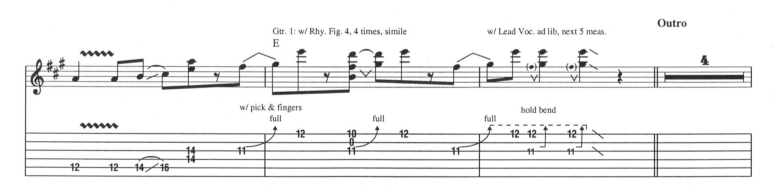

Norwegian Wood
(This Bird Has Flown)

Words and Music by John Lennon and Paul McCartney

All Gtrs.: Capo II

Intro

Moderately ♩. = 60

* Gtr. 1 (acous.)

(J.L.)

* Notes tabbed at 2nd fret played as open strings.

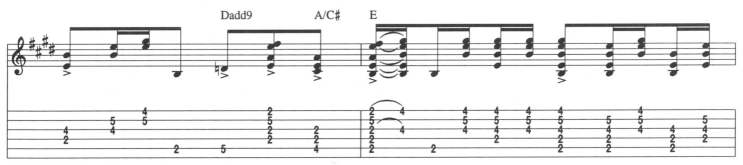

† Sitar arr. for Gtrs. 2 & 3
* Notes tabbed at 2nd fret played as open strings.

Verse

1. I once had a girl, or should I say she once had me. She showed me her

Rhy. Fig. 1

Rhy. Fig. 1A

Dadd9   A/C#   E

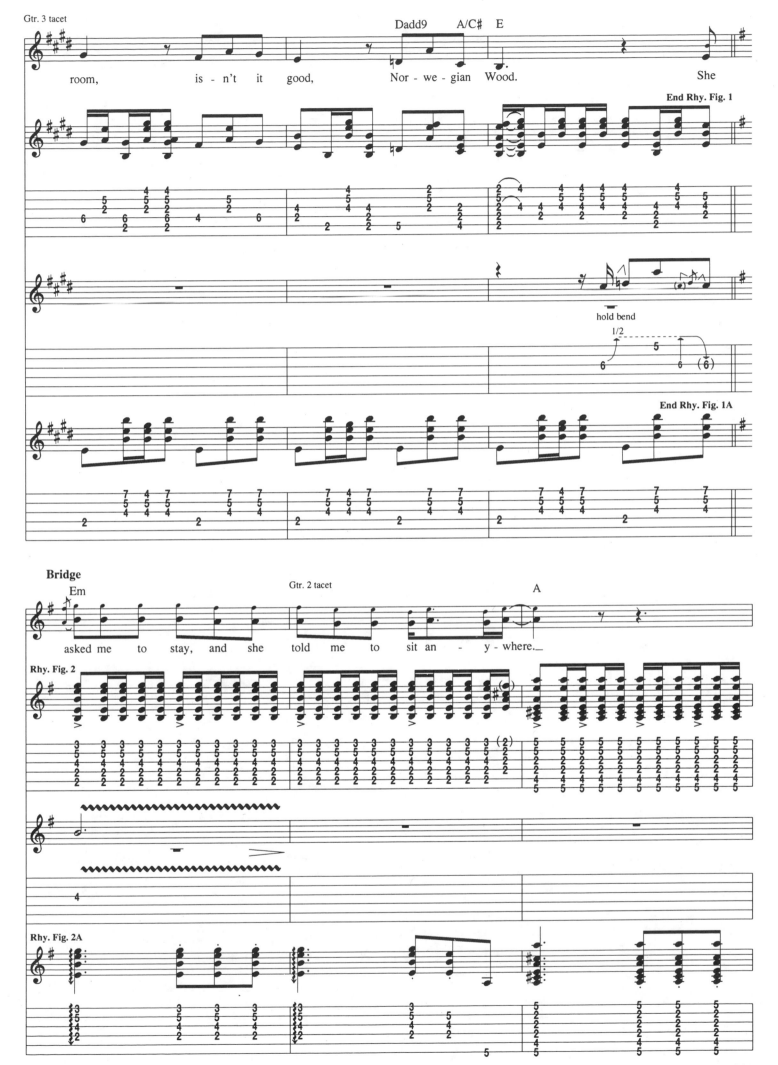

So   I looked a - round and I

no - ticed there was-n't   a chair. __

2. I   sat on a rug   bid - ing my time,   drink - ing her

Gtr. 1

Gtr. 4

End Rhy. Fig. 2

End Rhy. Fig. 2A

let ring

Verse
Gtrs. 1 & 4: w/ Rhy. Figs. 1 & 1A

Gtr. 2

120

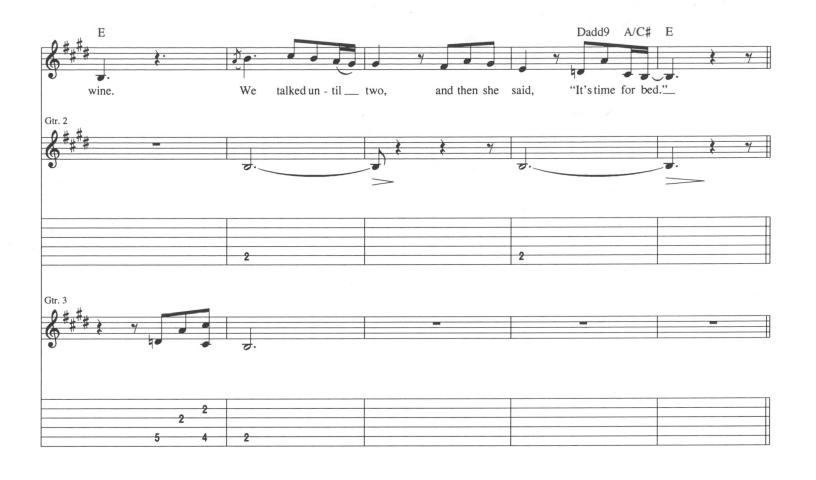

wine.   We talked un - til __ two,   and then she said,   "It's time for bed." __

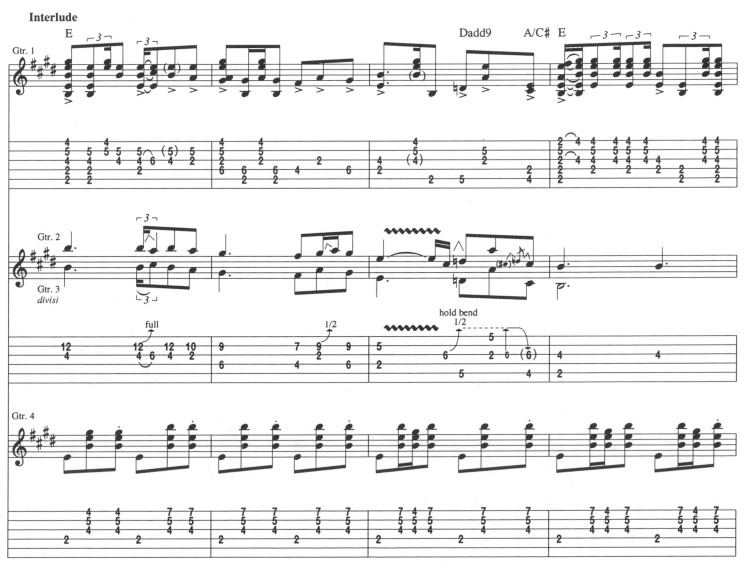

Interlude

Dadd9 Aadd6/C♯ E

She

Bridge
Gtrs. 2 & 3 tacet
Gtrs. 1 & 4: w/ Rhy. Figs. 2 & 2A

Em   A

told me she worked in the morn - ing and start-ed to laugh. ___   I

Em   F♯m7   B

told her I did-n't and crawled off to sleep in the bath. ___

Verse
Gtrs. 1 & 4: w/ Rhy. Figs. 1 & 1A

E   Dadd9   A/C♯

3. And   when I a - woke   I was a - lone, ___   this bird had

Gtr. 2

flown.   So   I lit a fire,   is- n't it good,   Nor-we-gian Wood.

Oh, Lonesome Me

Words and Music by Don Gibson

* Symbols in parentheses represent chord names respective to capoed gtr. and do not reflect actual sounding chords.

** Symbols in parentheses represent chord names respective to capoed guitar.
Symbols above reflect actual sounding chords. Capoed fret is "0" in tab.

Verse

1. Ev - 'ry - bod - y's _____ go - ing out and hav -

- ing fun. _____

I'm a fool _____ for stay - ing home _____ and

hav - ing none. _____ I

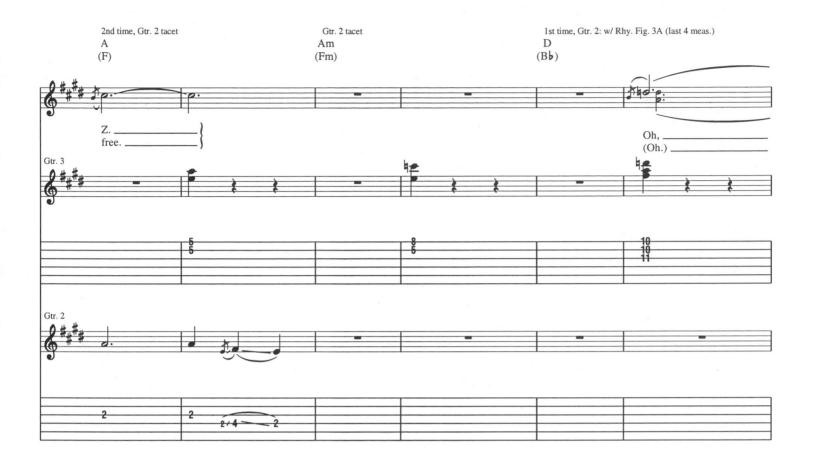

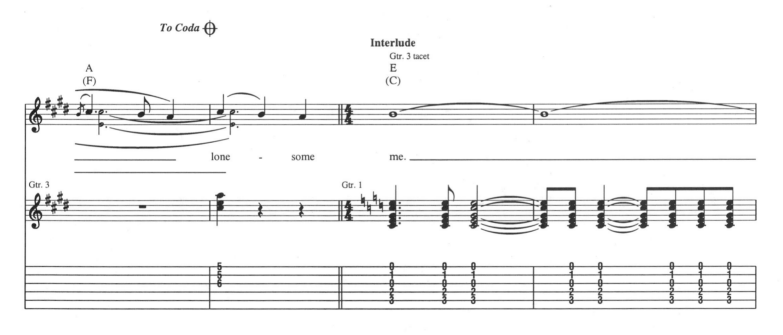

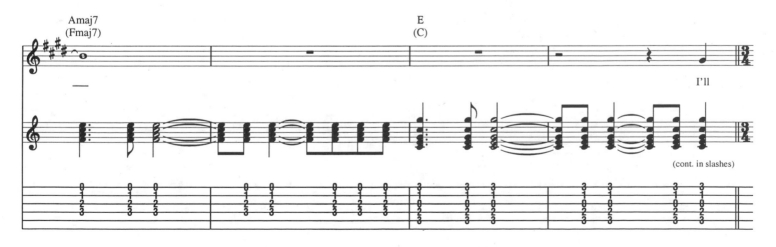

Bridge

bet she's   not   like   me,

she's out   and _____ fan - cy - free, _____

flirt - ing   with the   boys _____   with all   her

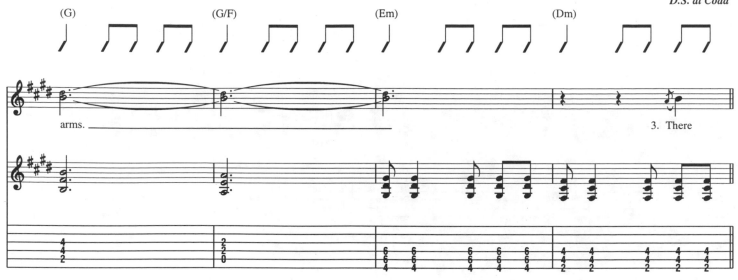

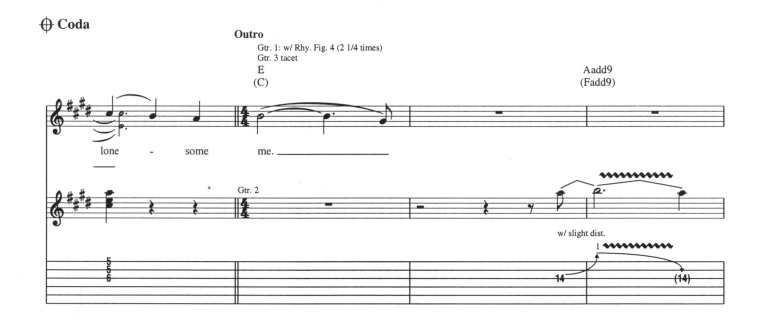

⊕ **Coda**

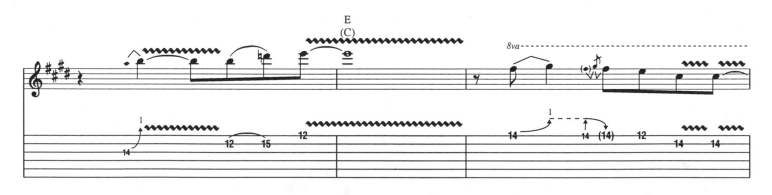

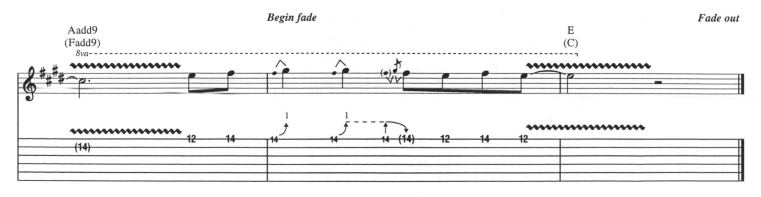

Our House

Words and Music by Graham Nash

Reason to Believe

Words and Music by Tim Hardin

Intro

Moderately slow, in 2 ♩ = 86

* Chord symbols reflect basic harmony.

1., 3. If I lis - ten long e - nough to you,
2. If I gave you time to change my mind,

I'd find a way ___ to leave, but it's all true,
I'd find a way ___ to leave the past be - hind,

know-ing   that you lied, __   straight - face   while I   cried.

To Coda 2 ⊕

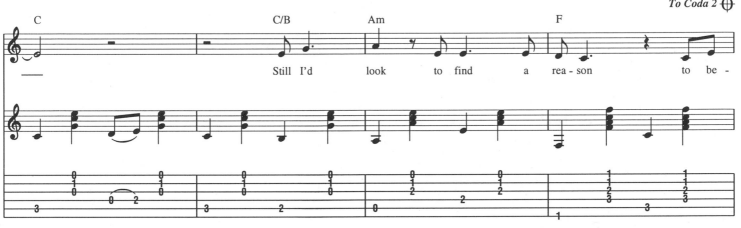

Still I'd   look   to find   a rea - son   to be -

To Coda 1 ⊕

Chorus

lieve.   Some - one like you   makes it hard to live _____

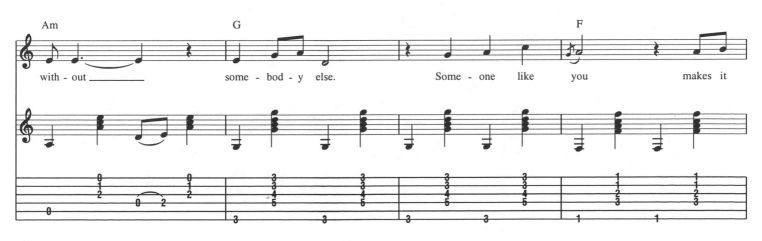

with - out ____   some - bod - y else.   Some - one like you   makes it

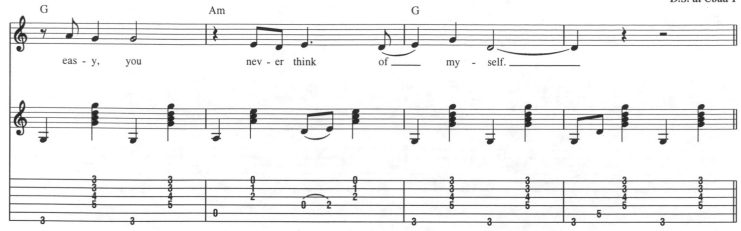

eas - y, you   nev - er think   of ____ my - self. ____

⊕ Coda 1

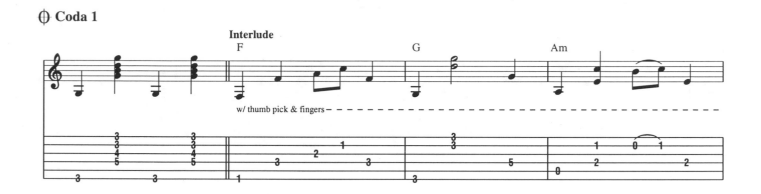

w/ thumb pick & fingers – – – – – –

w/ thumb pick & fingers – – – – – –

⊕ Coda 2

D.S. al Coda 2

w/ thumb pick – – – – – – –   w/ thumb pick & fingers – ⅂

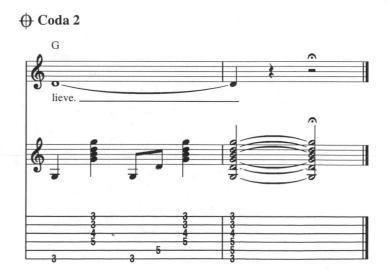

lieve. ____

She'd Rather Be With Me

Words and Music by Garry Bonner and Alan Gordon

Intro

Moderately ♩ = 128

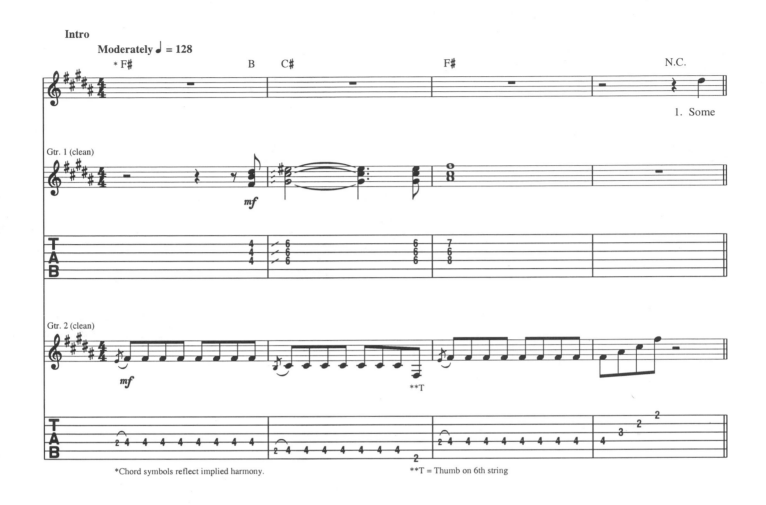

*Chord symbols reflect implied harmony.   **T = Thumb on 6th string

Verse

girls _____ love to run a - round, ___ love to han-dle ev-'ry-thing they see. ___ But my

girl   has more fun a - round, ___ and you know she's rath - er be with me. ___ Me, oh, my. _

But my girl (My girl.) has more fun a - round, and you

End Rhy. Fig. 3

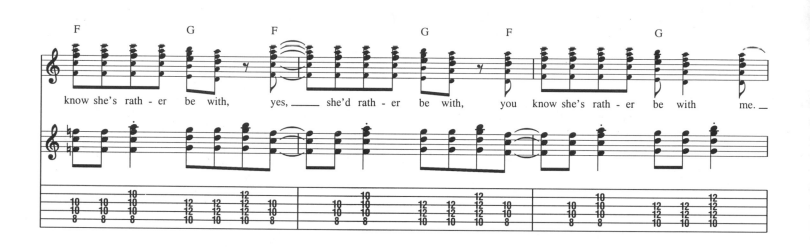

know she's rath - er be with, yes, she'd rath - er be with, you know she's rath - er be with me.

Outro
Gtr. 1: w/ Rhy. Fig. 3

Repeat and fade

Ah, you know she's rath - er be with me.

(Ra, ba, ba, ba, ba, ba, ba. (Ba, ba, ba.)
Ba, ba, ba, ba.)

140

Sweet Baby James

Words and Music by James Taylor

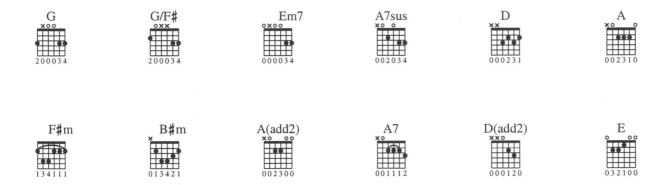

* Play bass notes with thumb, strum chords with index finger

is a young cow - boy, he lives on _____ the range.
first of De - cem - ber was cov - ered with snow.

His horse and his cat - tle ___ are his on - ly com - pan -

So was the turn - pike from Stock - bridge to Bos -

Strumming simile

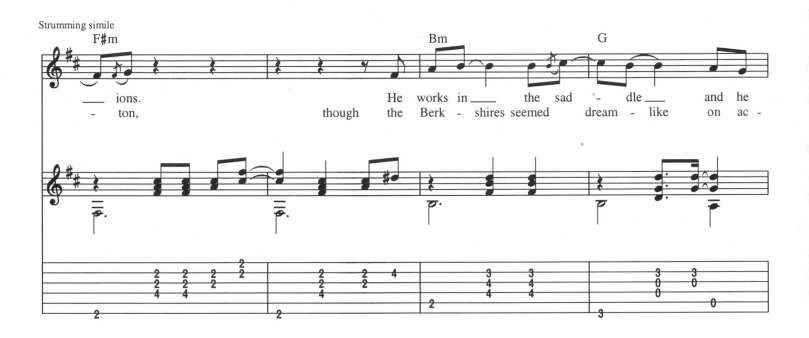

___ ions. He works in ___ the sad '- dle ___ and he

- ton, though the Berk - shires seemed dream - like on ac -

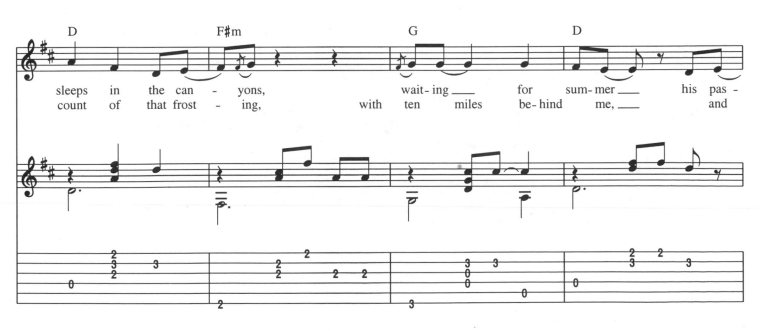

sleeps in the can - yons, wait - ing ___ for sum - mer ___ his pas -

count of that frost - ing, with ten miles be - hind me, ___ and

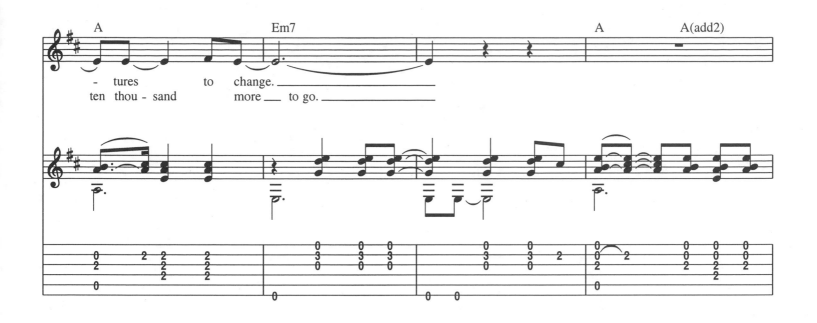

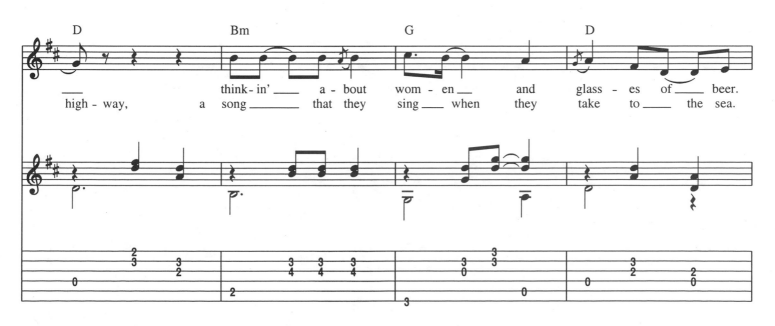

And clos - ing his eyes _ as the do - gies re - tire,
A song _ that they _ sing of their home _ in the sky.

He sings out a song _ which is _ soft but it's clear, _
May - be you can be - lieve it if it helps you to sleep, _

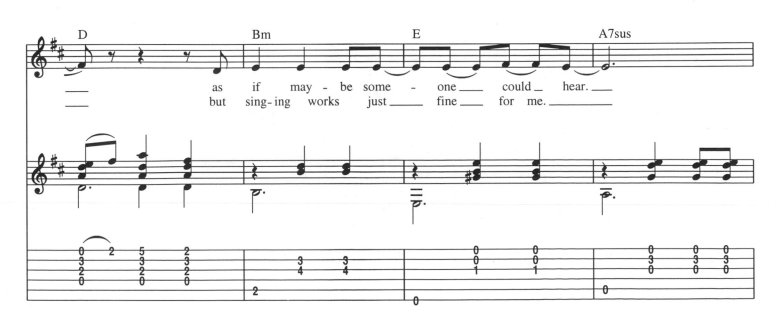

_ as if may - be some - one _ could _ hear. _
_ but sing-ing works just _ fine _ for me. _

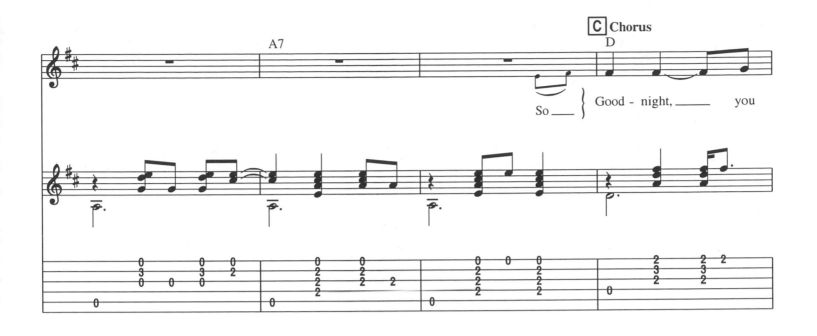

are the col - ors I choose. Won't you let me __ go - down__

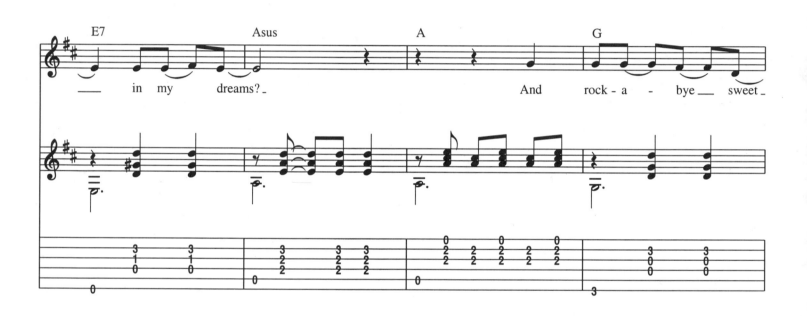

__ in my dreams? __ And rock - a - bye __ sweet

__ ba - by James. __ Now the

Take Me Home, Country Roads

Words and Music by John Denver, Bill Danoff and Taffy Nivert

*Chord symbols reflect implied tonality.

Blue Ridge Moun - tains, ___ Shen - an - do - ah Riv - er. ___
Min - er's la - dy, ___ Stran - ger to blue wa - ter. ___

simile on repeat

let ring

___ Life is old ___ there, ___ old - er than the ___
___ Dark and dust - y, ___ paint - ed on ___ the ___

let ring

trees, young - er than the moun - tains, grow - in' like a breeze.
sky, mist - y taste of moon - shine, tear - drop on my

let ring

played 1st time only

𝄋 Chorus

Coun - try roads, take me home

eye.

simile on repeats
*let ring throughout

played 1st time only

*next 16 meas.

to the place _____ I be - long: _____

West Vir - gin - ia, _____ moun - tain mom - ma. _____

Take _ me home, _____ coun - try roads. _____

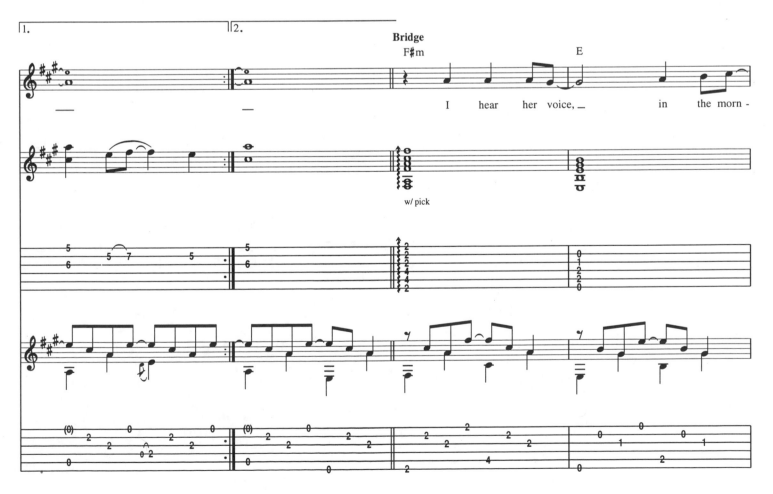

Bridge

I hear her voice, _ in the morn -

w/ pick

-in' hour ___ she calls ___ me. The ra - di - o ___ re - minds ___ me of my

let ring _____

home far a - way. ___ And driv - in' down ___ the road ___ I get a feel -

let ring _____

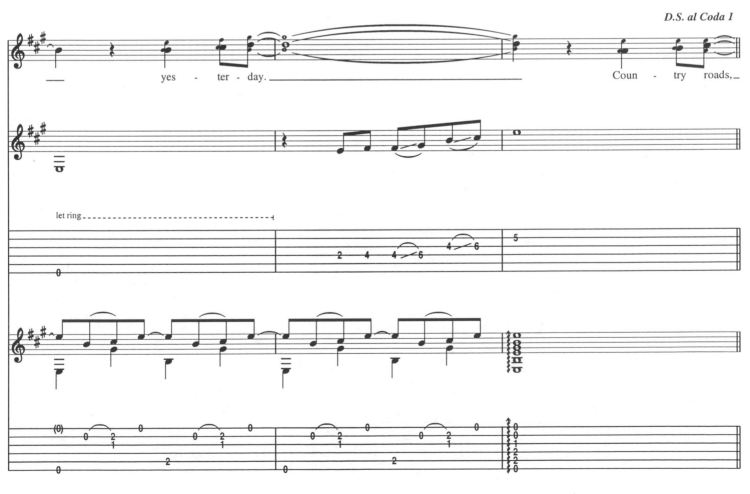

153

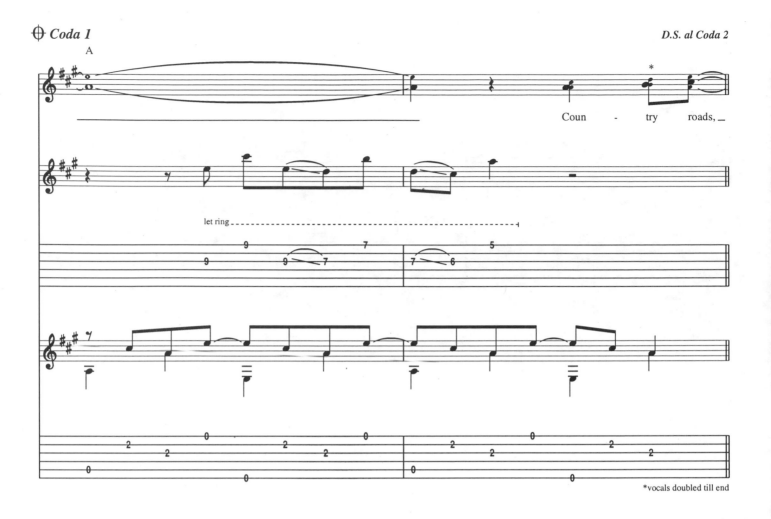

D.S. al Coda 2

Coun - try roads, ___

*vocals doubled till end

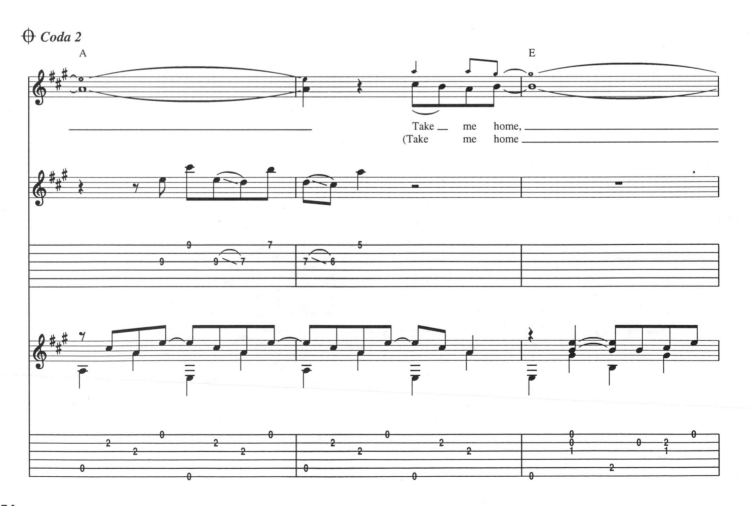

Take ___ me home, ___
(Take ___ me home ___

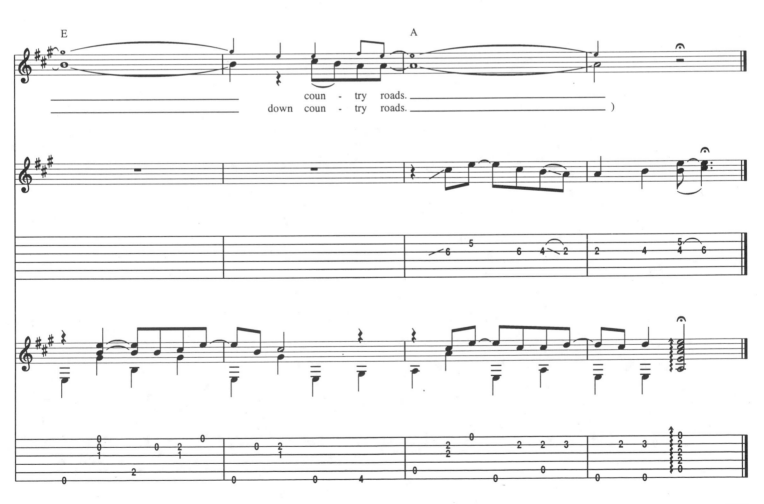

Teach Your Children

Words and Music by Graham Nash

and know they love _____ you.

End Rhy. Fig. 3

2. And

Verse
Gtr. 2: w/ Rhy. Fig. 2, 2 times, simile

you ____ of ____ the ten - der years ____ can't know ____ the fears that your eld - ers grew ____

(Can you hear? _____ Do you care? _____ Can you see you

* vol. swells

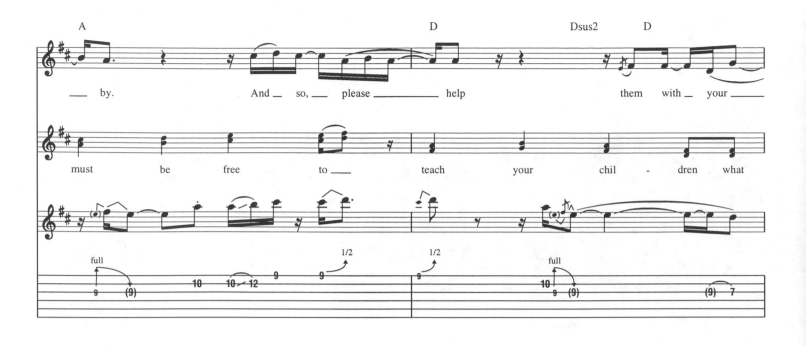

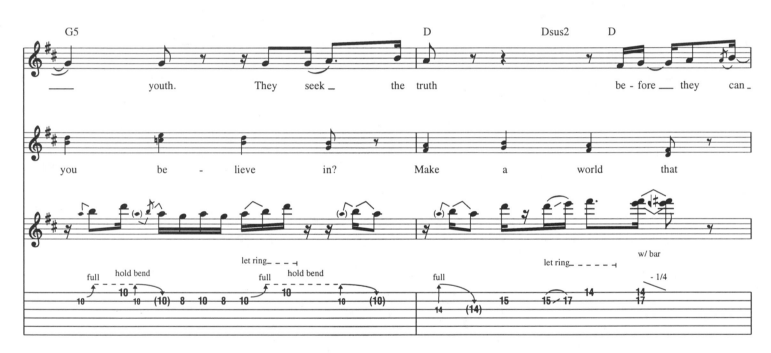

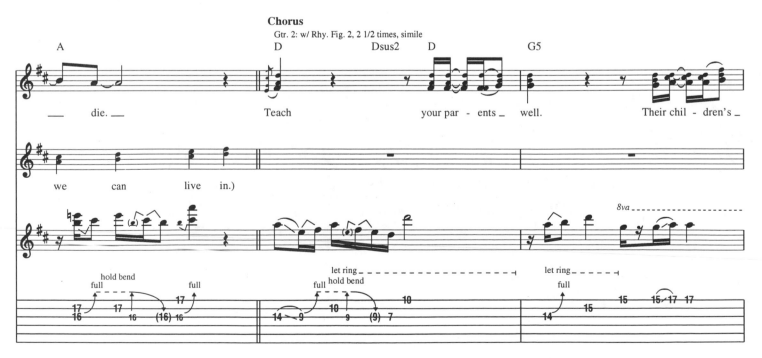

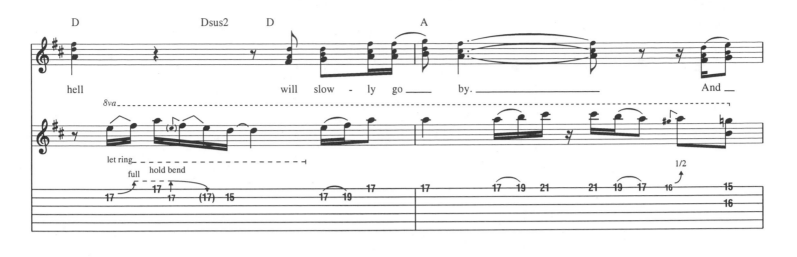

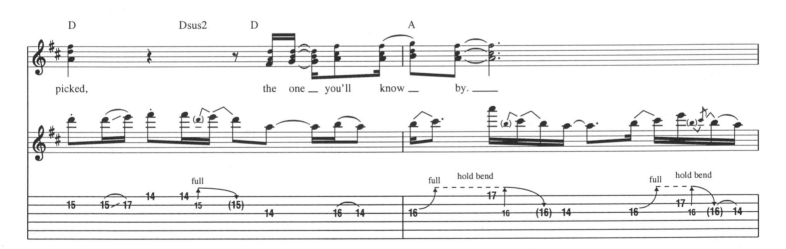

Gtr. 2: w/ Rhy. Fig. 3, simile

cry.   So just   look at   them_ and   sigh. _____   and know they

love ____ you. ____

This Land Is Your Land

Words and Music by Woody Guthrie

* Two gtrs. arr. for one.   ** Symbols in parentheses represent chord names respective to capoed guitar.
Symbols above reflect actual sounding chords. Capoed fret is "0" in tab.

† T = Thumb on 6th string

for - est   to the Gulf Stream wat - ers, _____

this land   was made _ for you and me.   1. As I ____ went

End Rhy. Fig. 1   **Rhy. Fig. 2**   **End Rhy. Fig. 2**

𝄋 Verse

Gtr. 1: w/ Rhy. Fig. 1
3rd time, Gtr. 2: w/ Fill 1

walk - ing _____ that rib - bon of high - way,
ram - bled _____ and I fol - lowed my foot - steps
shin - ing _____ as I ____ was stroll - ing,

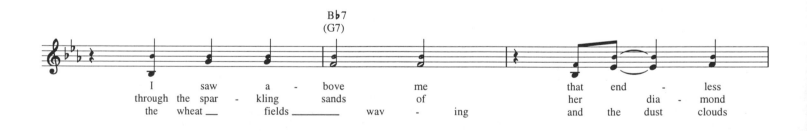

I saw a - bove me that end - less
through the spar - kling sands of her dia - mond
the wheat __ fields _____ wav - ing and the dust clouds

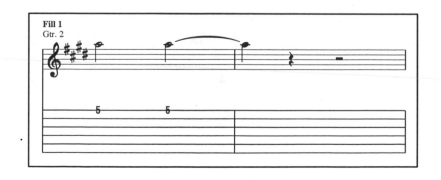

Fill 1
Gtr. 2

* Symbols in double parentheses reflect chord names respective to Gtr. 2.

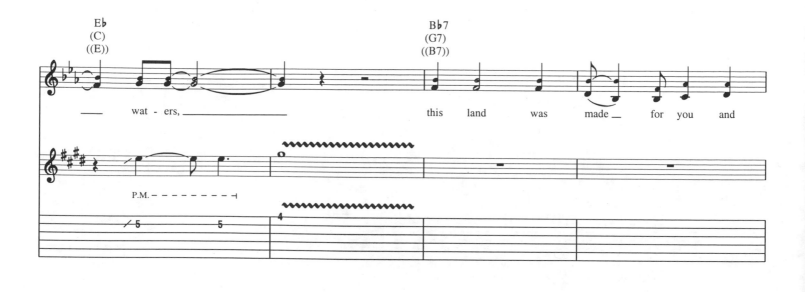

Coda 2

Outro

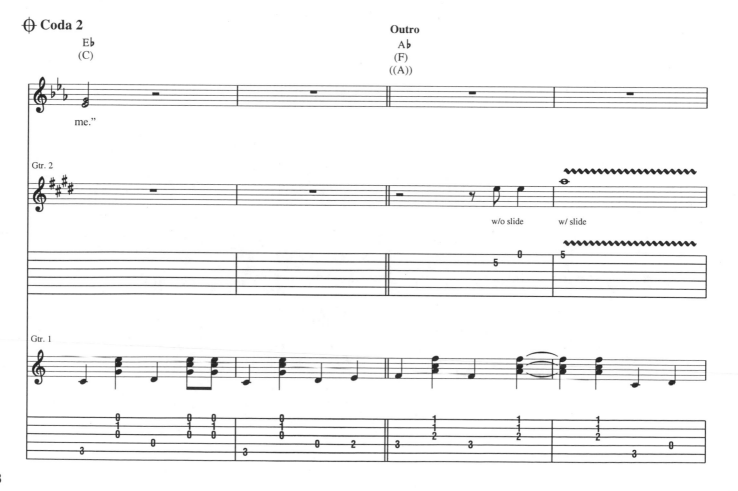

Time in a Bottle

Words and Music by Jim Croce

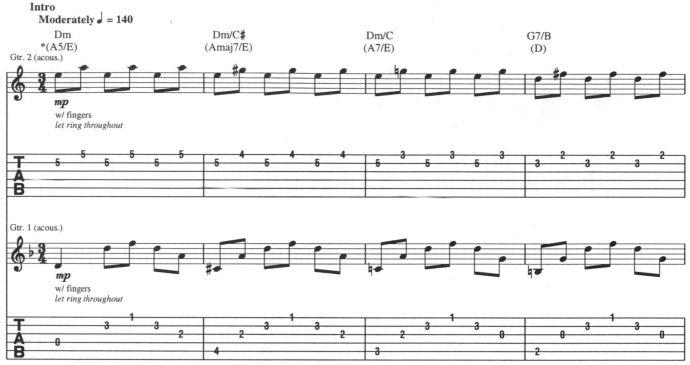

*Symbols in parentheses represent chord names respective to capoed guitar.
Symbols above reflect actual sounding chord. Capoed fret is "0" in tab.

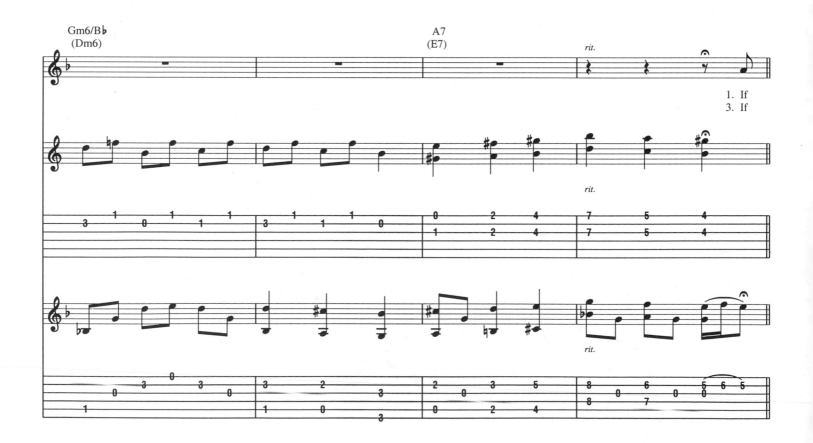

save ev -'ry - day 'til e - ter - ni - ty ____ pass - es a - way,_
save ev -'ry - day like a treas - ure and then ____ a -
box would be emp - ty ex - cept for the mem - 'ry of how __

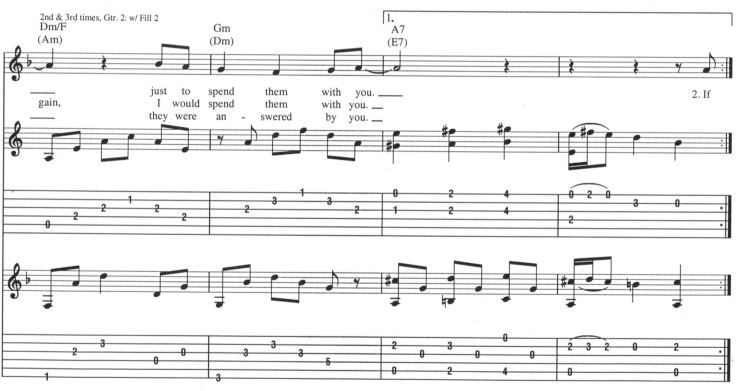

____ gain, just to spend them with you. ____
gain, I would spend them with you. ____
they were an - swered by you. ____

2. If

Gtrs. 1 & 2: w/ Riffs A & A1

looked a - round e - nough ___ to know ___ that you're the one I

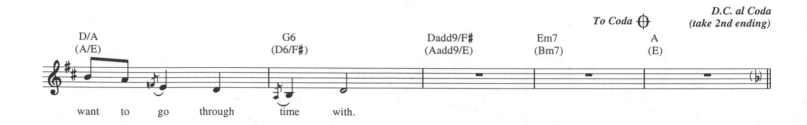

want to go through time with.

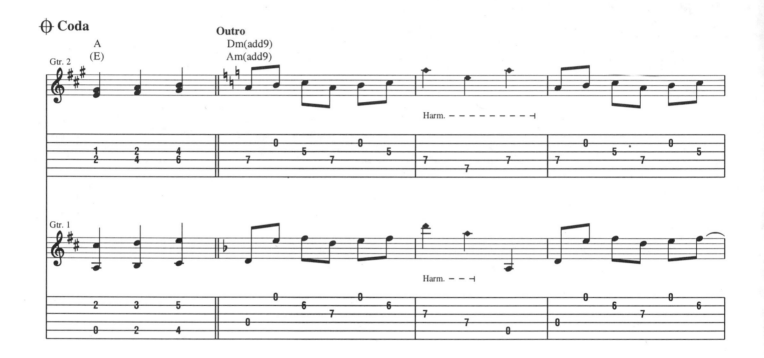

Turn! Turn! Turn!

(To Everything There Is a Season)

Words from the Book of Ecclesiastes
Adaption and Music by Pete Seeger

* Chord symbols reflect combined tonality.

*Vocs. doubled throughout

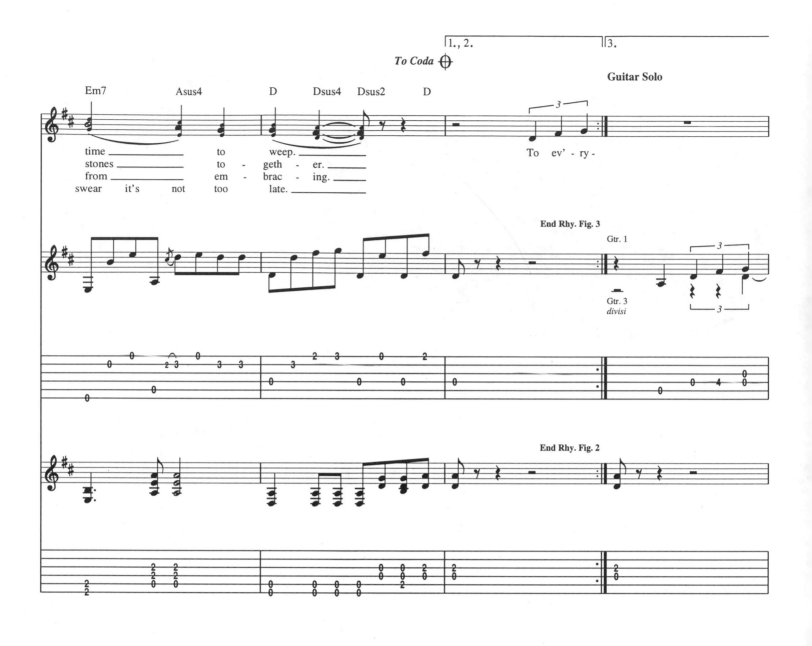

Coda

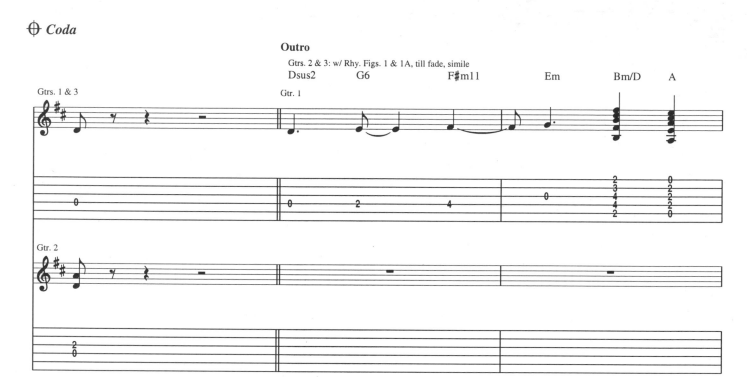

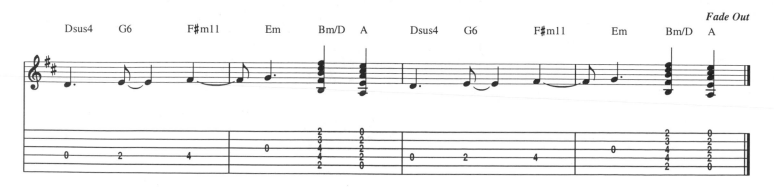

180

Up on the Roof

Words and Music by Gerry Goffin and Carole King

Gtr. 1: Capo III

*Symbols in parentheses represent chord names repsective to capoed guitar. Symbols above reflect actual sounding chords.
Capoed fret is "0" in tab. Chord symbols reflect implied harmony.

*Vol. swell

**Composite arr. of piano & gtr., next 8 meas.

Verse

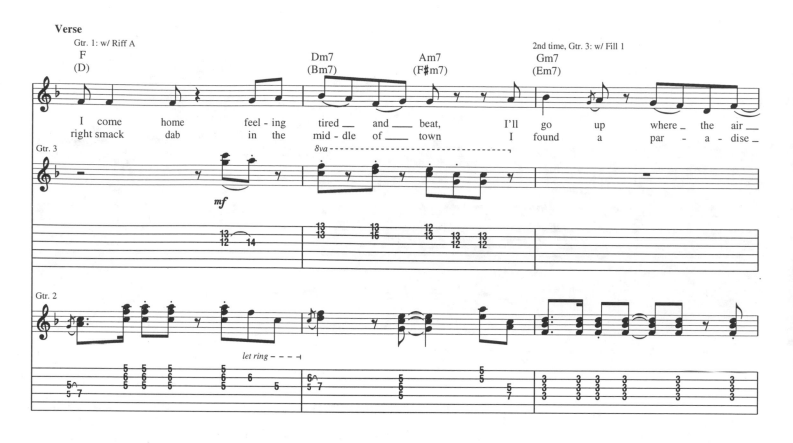

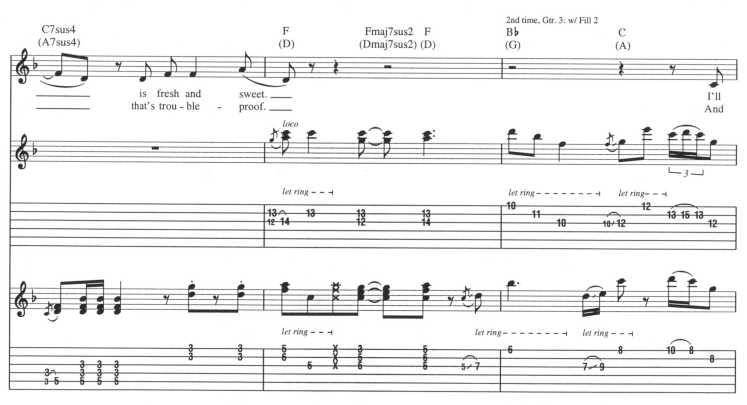

get far a - way from the hus - tl - ing ___ crowd and all ___ that rat - race noise __
if this old world starts a get - ting you ___ down there's room e - nough for two ___

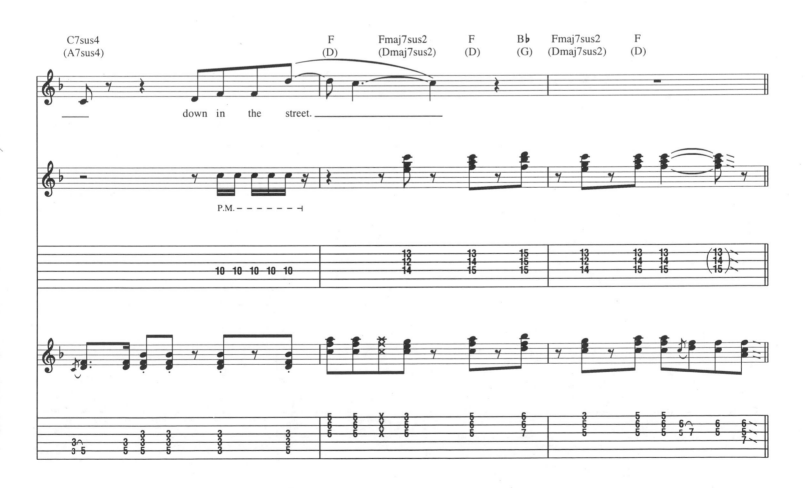

down in the street. ___

Chorus

Gtr. 1: w/ Riff B
Gtr. 2: w/ Rhy. Fig. 1
Gtr. 3: w/ Riff B1

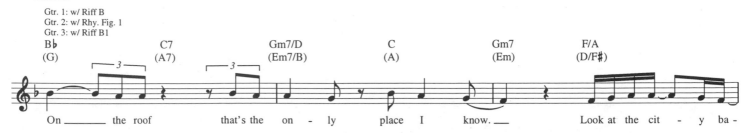

On _____ the roof   that's the   on - ly   place I   know. _____   Look at the cit - y ba-

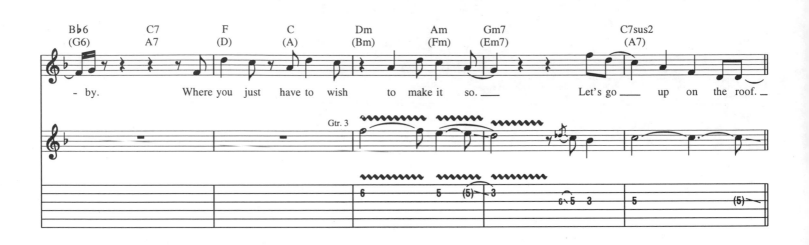

- by.   Where you just   have to   wish   to make it   so. _____   Let's go _____   up   on   the roof.

Interlude

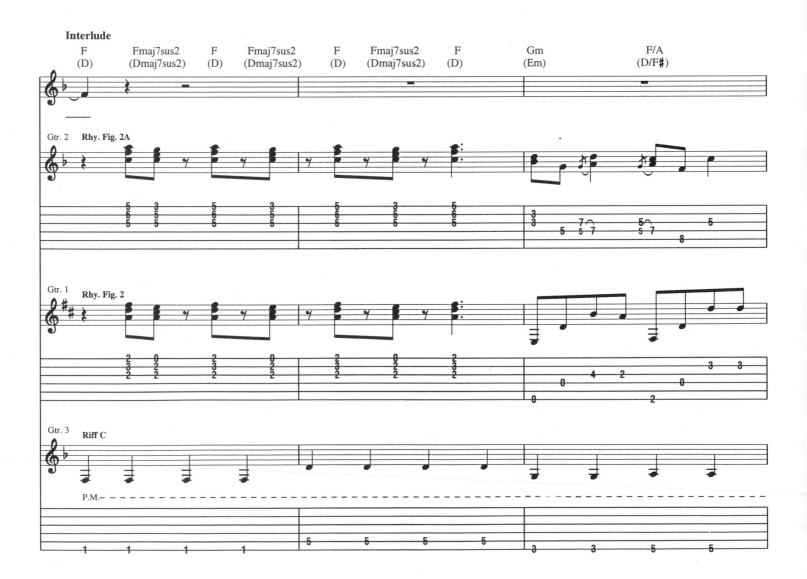

186

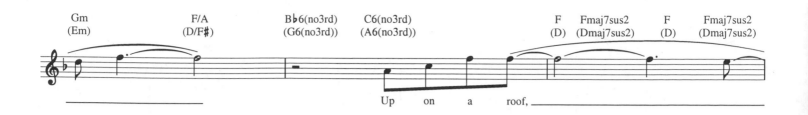

Up on a roof,

oh, _____ now. _____

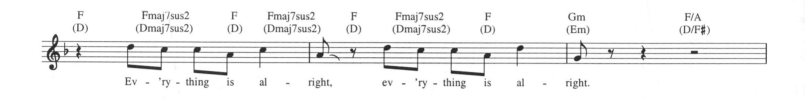

Ev - 'ry - thing is al - right, ev - 'ry - thing is al - right.

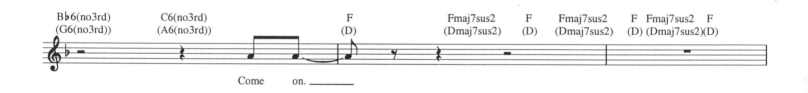

Come on. _____

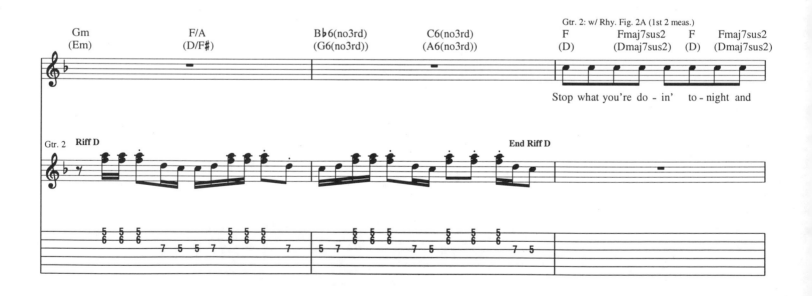

Gtr. 2: w/ Rhy. Fig. 2A (1st 2 meas.)

Stop what you're do - in' to - night and

Gtr. 2 **Riff D**   **End Riff D**

Gtr. 2: w/ Riff D

climb up the stairs with me and see me.   We got the

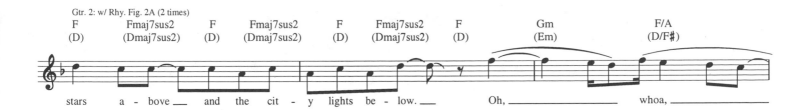

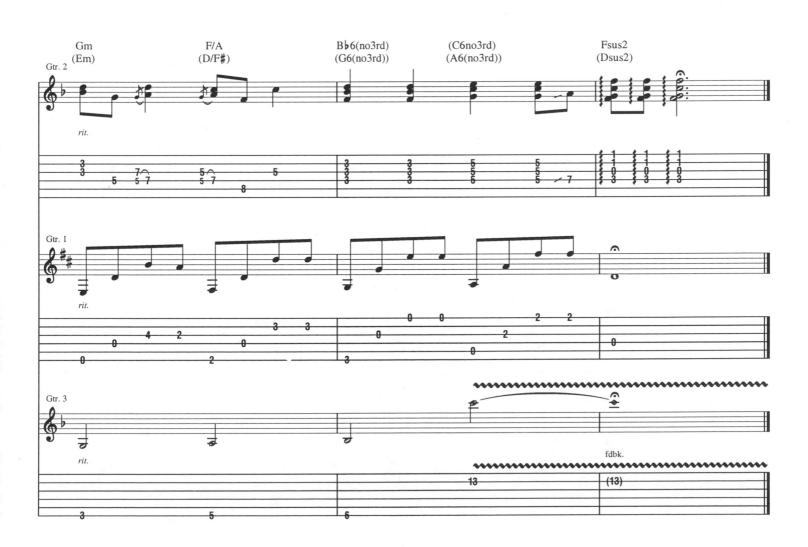

We Shall Overcome

Musical and Lyrical Adaptation by Zilphia Horton, Frank Hamilton, Guy Carawan and Pete Seeger
Inspired by African American Gospel Singing, members of the Food and Tobacco Workers Union,
Charleston, SC, and the southern Civil Rights Movement

Additional Lyrics

3. We shall live in peace.
    We shall live in peace.
    We shall live in peace someday.
    Whoa...

4. We shall all be free.
    We shall all be free.
    We shall all be free someday.
    Whoa...

5. We are not afraid.
    We are not afraid.
    We are not afraid today.
    Whoa...

6. We shall overcome.
    We shall overcome.
    We shall overcome someday.
    Oh...

Wild World

Words and Music by Cat Stevens

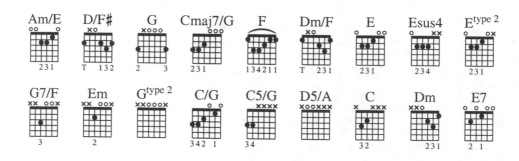

Intro
Moderately slow

La, la, la, la, la, la, la, la, __ la, la. __ La, la, la, la, la, la, la, la, __ la, la. __

__ La, la, la, la, la, la, la, la, __ la, la, __ la.

Verse

1. Now that I've lost __ ev - 'ry-thing to __ you __ you say you want to start some - thing __
2. You know I've seen a lot of what the world can __ do __ and it's break-in' my heart __ in __

new. __ And it's break-in' my heart __ you're leav - in', ba - by, I'm griev - in'.
two __ be-cause I nev - er want to see you sad, __ girl. __ Don't be a bad __ girl. __

But if you want to leave ____ take good care. _ Hope you have a lot of nice things to wear,_
But if you want to leave ____ take good care. _ Hope you have a lot of nice friends out

_____ but, then a lot of nice things turn _ bad out there._
there,_ but just re-mem-ber there's a lot of bad and be-ware._ Well, ____

Chorus

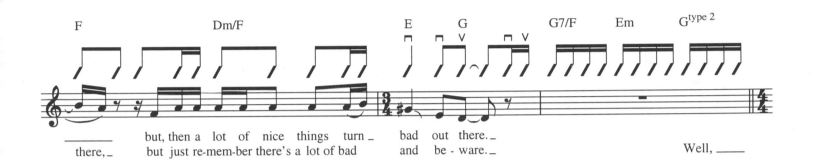

Oo,
oo, ba - by, ba - by, it's a wild world. ____

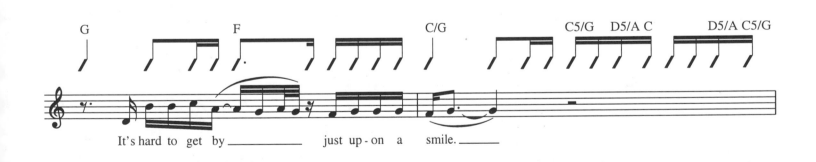

It's hard to get by ____ just up-on a smile. ____

Oo, ba - by, ba - by, it's a wild world. ____

1.
G   F   C/G   Dm   E7

I'll al-ways re-mem-ber you ___ like a child, girl. ___

2.
G   F   C/G   Dm   E7

And I'll al-ways re-mem-ber you ___ like a child, ___ girl. _____

Interlude-Verse

Am/E   D/F#   G   Cmaj7/G

La, la, la, la, la, la, la, la, ___ la, la. _

F   Dm/F   E   Esus4   E type 2

La, la, la, la, la, la, la, la, ___ la, la, la.   3. Ba-by, I love ___ you, ___

Am/E   D/F#   G   Cmaj7/G

but if you want to leave ___ take good ___ care. _   Hope you make a lot of nice friends out

F   Dm/F   E   G   G7/F   Em   G type 2

there. _ But just re-mem-ber there's a lot of bad and _ be-ware. _   Well,

Chorus

oo, ba - by, ba - by, it's a wild world. _____

{ It's / And it's } hard to get by _____ just up - on a smile. _____

Oo, ba - by, ba - by, it's a wild world. _____

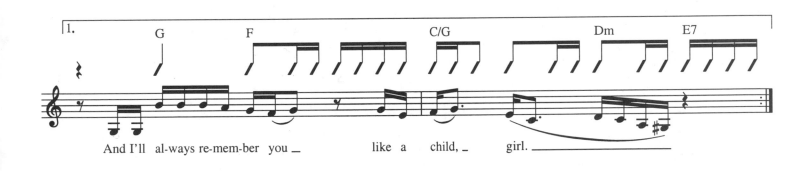

And I'll al - ways re - mem - ber you _____ like a child, _ girl. _____

And I'll al - ways re - mem - ber you _____ like a child, girl. _____

You're Only Lonely

Words and Music by John David Souther

(Oo.   )

Verse

1. When the world is read-y to fall _____ on your lit-tle shoul--ders, and when you're feel-in' lone-ly and ___ small, _____ you need some-bod-y there to hold _____ you. Well, you can call out my name _____ when you're on-ly lone-ly. Now don't you ev-er be a-shamed; _____ you're on-ly lone-

(Oo.   )

Verse

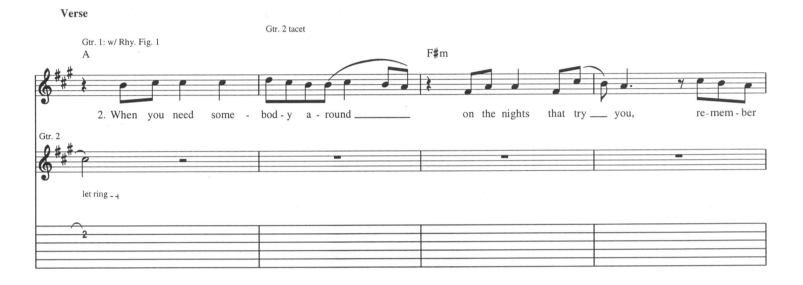

2. When you need some-bod-y a-round ___ on the nights that try ___ you, re-mem-ber

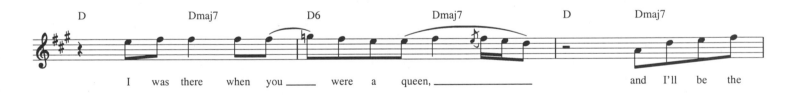

I was there when you ___ were a queen, ___ and I'll be the

last one there be-side ___ you. ___ So you can call out my name ___

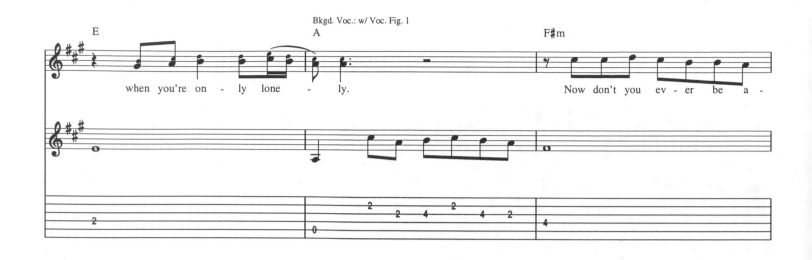

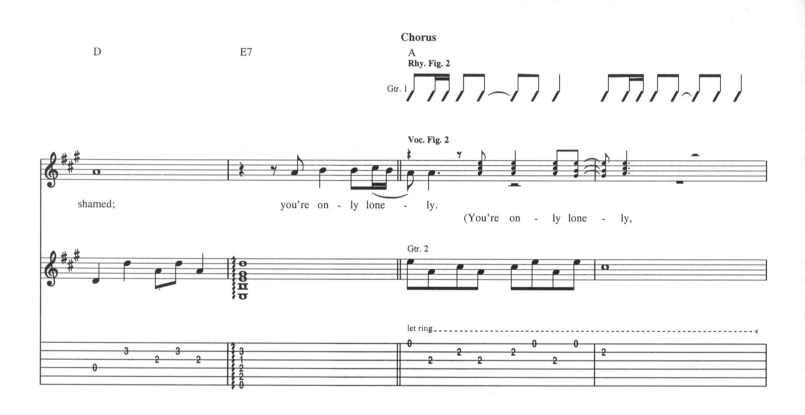

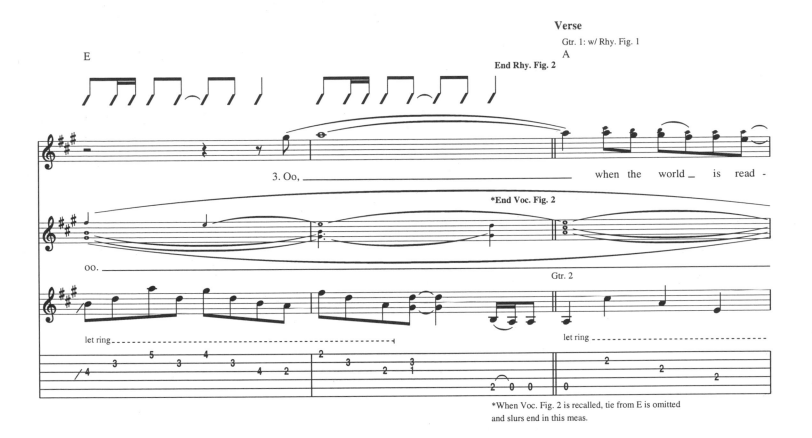

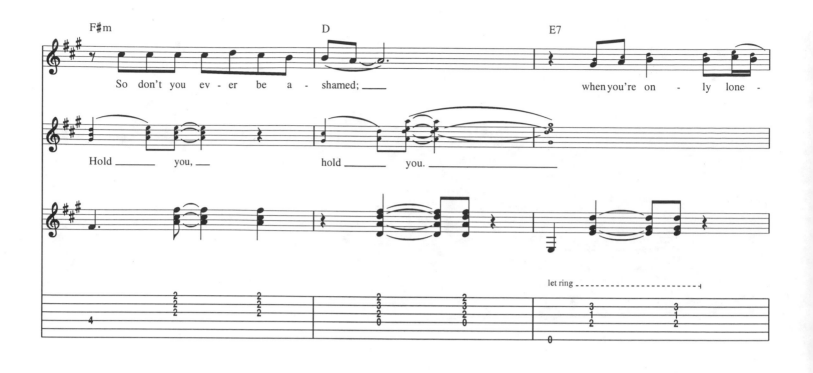

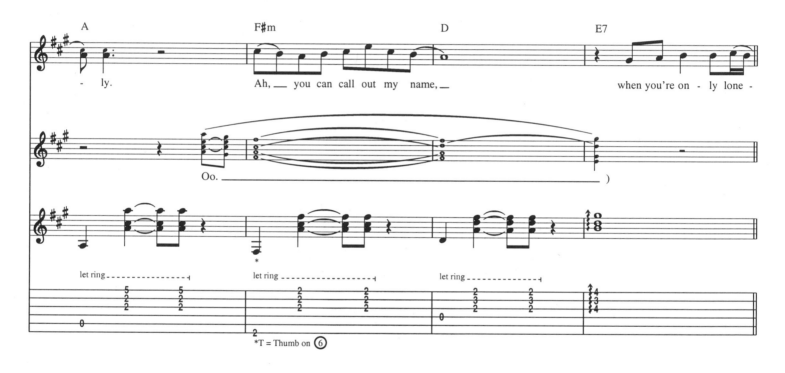

*T = Thumb on ⑥

Outro-Chorus

Gtr. 1: w/ Rhy. Fig. 2, till fade

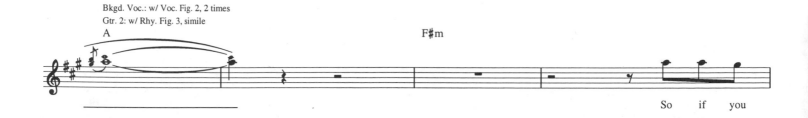

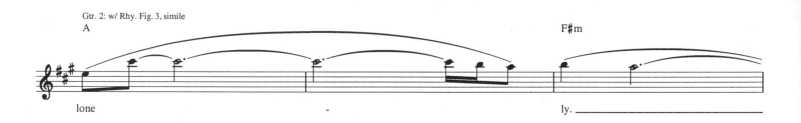

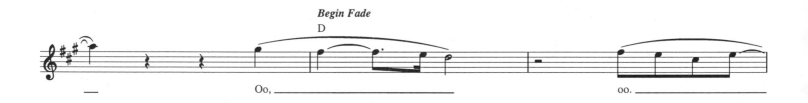

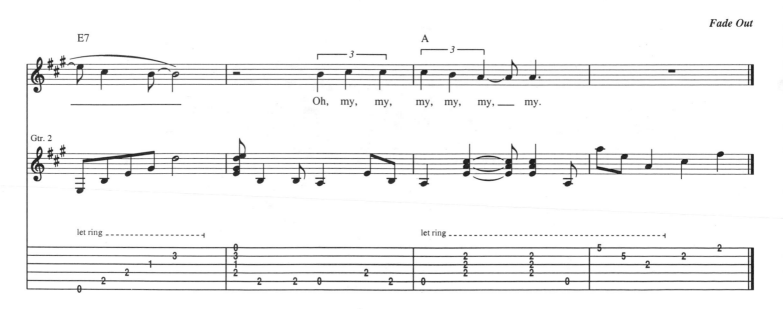

You've Got a Friend

Words and Music by Carole King

*Symbols in parentheses represent chord names respective to capoed guitar.
Symbols above reflect actual sounding chord. Capoed fret is "0" in TAB.

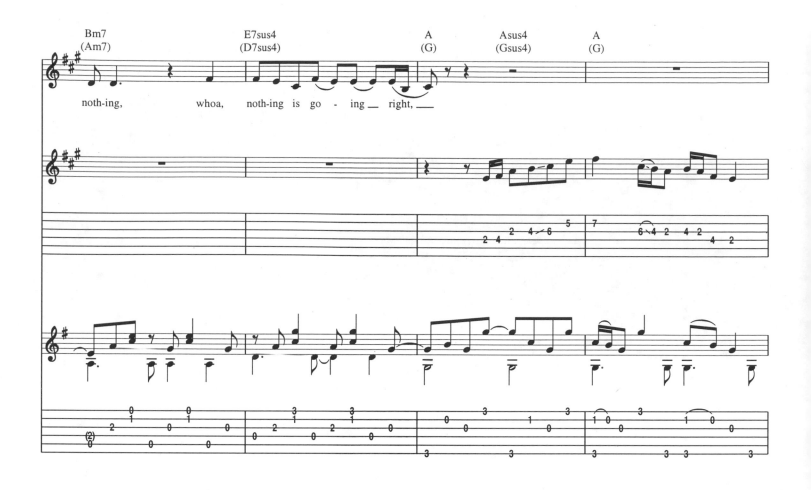

noth-ing,   whoa,   noth-ing is go - ing — right, ___

close   your eyes _ and think of me,   and soon I will _ be   there _   to

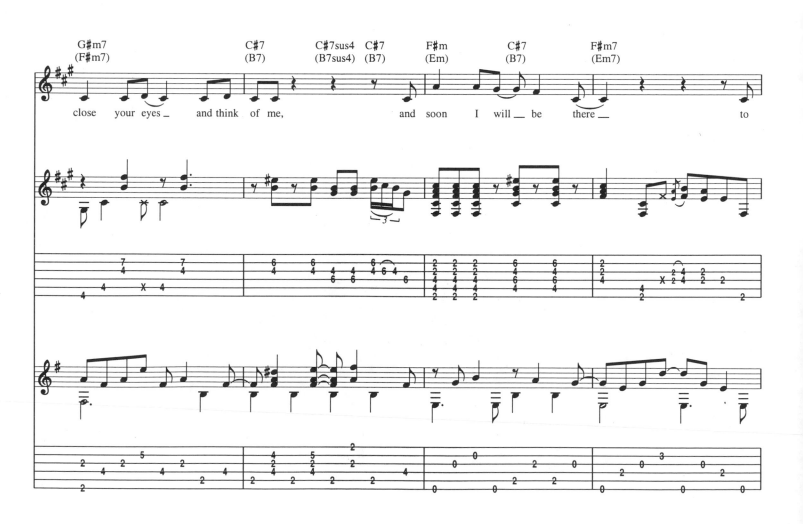

bright-en up   e - ven your dark - est   night.___   You just   call___

Chorus

___   out my ___ name, ___   and you know wher-ev - er I am, ___   I'll come   run -

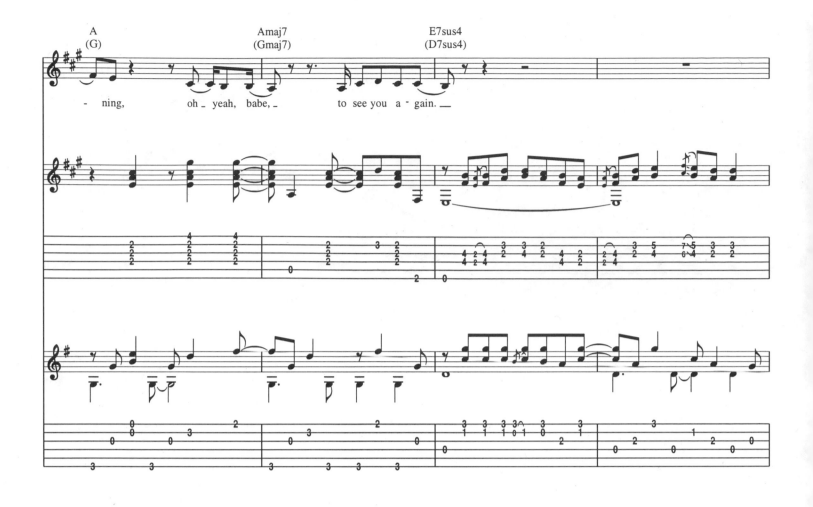

-ning,   oh _ yeah, babe, _   to see you a - gain. _

Win-ter, spring, sum-mer or fall, _   now, all you got to do _ is _ call, _   and I'll

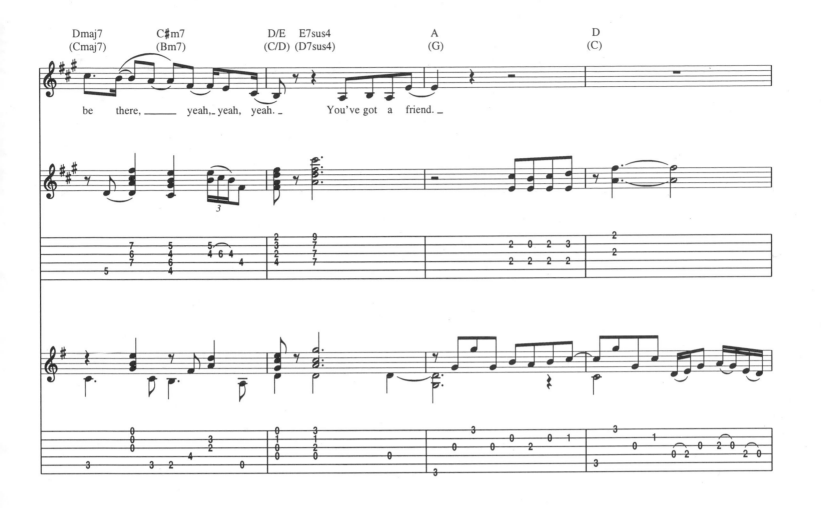

be there, _____ yeah,_ yeah, yeah._ You've got a friend._

2. If the sky _____ a - bove _____ you should turn_

208

hurt you __ and de- sert __ you. Well, they'll take your soul __ if you let __ them, oh yeah, but don't __

Chorus

__ you __ let them. You just call __ out my name, __ and you
(Call __ out my name, and you

all you've got to do is call. ___ Lord, I'll be ___ there, ___ yes I will. ___

Outro

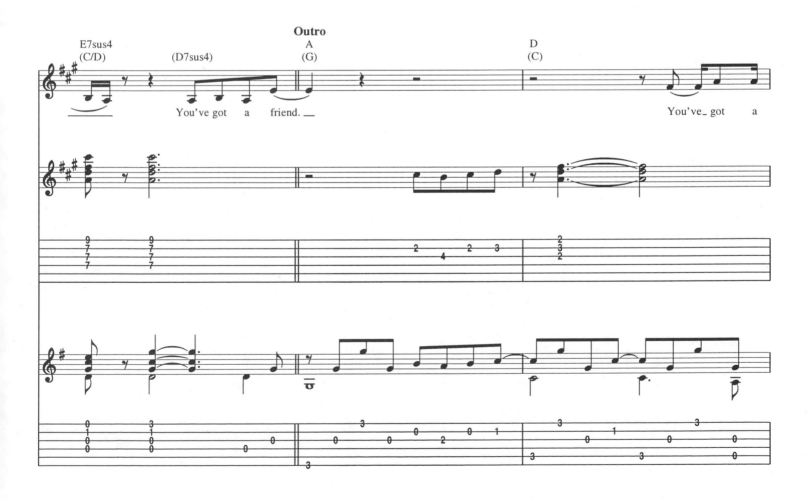

You've got a friend. ___ You've got a

friend, _ yeah. _ Ain't it good_to know you've got _ a friend?_ Ain't it good_ to know you've got a friend?_

Oh, yeah, _ yeah. _ You've got a friend. _

Guitar Notation Legend

Guitar Music can be notated three different ways: on a *musical staff*, in *tablature*, and in *rhythm slashes*.

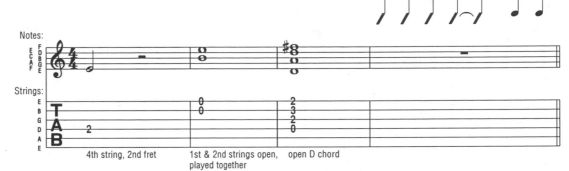

RHYTHM SLASHES are written above the staff. Strum chords in the rhythm indicated. Use the chord diagrams found at the top of the first page of the transcription for the appropriate chord voicings. Round noteheads indicate single notes.

THE MUSICAL STAFF shows pitches and rhythms and is divided by bar lines into measures. Pitches are named after the first seven letters of the alphabet.

TABLATURE graphically represents the guitar fingerboard. Each horizontal line represents a string, and each number represents a fret.

HALF-STEP BEND: Strike the note and bend up 1/2 step.

WHOLE-STEP BEND: Strike the note and bend up one step.

GRACE NOTE BEND: Strike the note and bend up as indicated. The first note does not take up any time.

SLIGHT (MICROTONE) BEND: Strike the note and bend up 1/4 step.

BEND AND RELEASE: Strike the note and bend up as indicated, then release back to the original note. Only the first note is struck.

PRE-BEND: Bend the note as indicated, then strike it.

VIBRATO: The string is vibrated by rapidly bending and releasing the note with the fretting hand.

WIDE VIBRATO: The pitch is varied to a greater degree by vibrating with the fretting hand.

HAMMER-ON: Strike the first (lower) note with one finger, then sound the higher note (on the same string) with another finger by fretting it without picking.

PULL-OFF: Place both fingers on the notes to be sounded. Strike the first note and without picking, pull the finger off to sound the second (lower) note.

LEGATO SLIDE: Strike the first note and then slide the same fret-hand finger up or down to the second note. The second note is not struck.

SHIFT SLIDE: Same as legato slide, except the second note is struck.

TRILL: Very rapidly alternate between the notes indicated by continuously hammering on and pulling off.

TAPPING: Hammer ("tap") the fret indicated with the pick-hand index or middle finger and pull off to the note fretted by the fret hand.

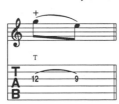

NATURAL HARMONIC: Strike the note while the fret-hand lightly touches the string directly over the fret indicated.

PINCH HARMONIC: The note is fretted normally and a harmonic is produced by adding the edge of the thumb or the tip of the index finger of the pick hand to the normal pick attack.

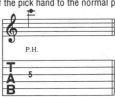

PICK SCRAPE: The edge of the pick is rubbed down (or up) the string, producing a scratchy sound.

MUFFLED STRINGS: A percussive sound is produced by laying the fret hand across the string(s) without depressing, and striking them with the pick hand.

PALM MUTING: The note is partially muted by the pick hand lightly touching the string(s) just before the bridge.

RAKE: Drag the pick across the strings indicated with a single motion.

TREMOLO PICKING: The note is picked as rapidly and continuously as possible.

VIBRATO BAR DIVE AND RETURN: The pitch of the note or chord is dropped a specified number of steps (in rhythm) then returned to the original pitch.

VIBRATO BAR SCOOP: Depress the bar just before striking the note, then quickly release the bar.

VIBRATO BAR DIP: Strike the note and then immediately drop a specified number of steps, then release back to the original pitch.

215

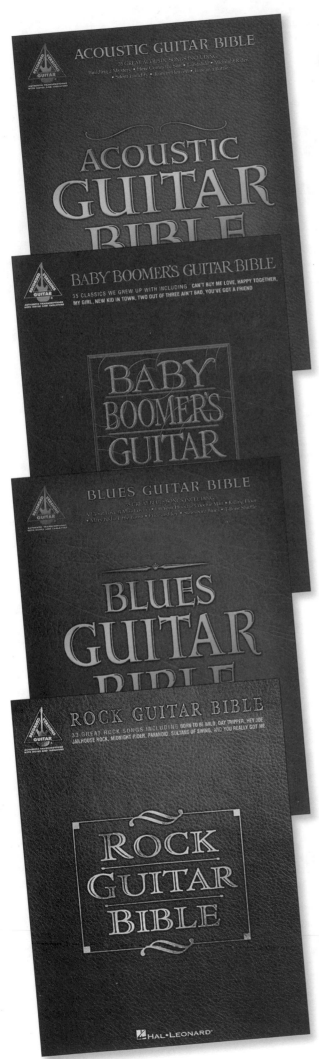